12 Circular Walks Around
CROMFORD & HIGH PEAK RAILWAY
Whaley Bridge to Cromford

Written and Published by
Brian Bethune & Dave Singleton.
Copyright 2016.

ISBN No. 0 9525288 3 5

Design and Print by Printexpress (Buxton) Ltd.
The Old Schoolhouse, Market Street, Buxton, SK17 6LD.

No part of this book may be reproduced in any
form without the express written consent of the authors.

CONTENTS

Page Nos.

Walk Talk   4

Two Blokes, a Book and a Railway   6

Walking Along a Piece of History   8

WALK 1	Whaley Bridge – Fernilee 6.75 miles / 10.9km	14
WALK 2	Fernilee Reservoir 2.95 miles / 4.75km	23
WALK 3	Bunsal Incline – Burbage Tunnel 3.75 miles / 6.2km	27
WALK 4	Grinlow – Ladmanlow 4.05 miles / 6.5km	33
WALK 5	Grinlow – Brierlow 9.75 miles / 15.3km	39
WALK 6	Chelmorton – Hindlow 5.28 miles / 8.5km	47
WALK 7	Hurdlow – Pilsbury Castle 9.6 miles / 15.5km	54
WALK 8	Parsley Hay – Newhaven Crossing 8.25 miles / 13.28km	60
WALK 9	Minninglow – Roystone Grange 8 miles / 13km	68

WALK 10	Brassington – Longcliffe 8.9 miles / 14.3km	75
WALK 11	Middleton Top - Harboro Rocks 5.6 miles / 9km	81
WALK 12	High Peak Junction – Middleton Top 7.38 miles / 11.9km	89

Acknowledgements	100
References	101
Places of Interest	102
C&HPR Line of 1831	104
Map Symbols	Inside Back Cover

Walk Talk

On the Trail of an Old Railway

In 2006, Brian Bethune devised eight walks for the Chapel-en-le-Frith Rambling Club. Now, in collaboration with Dave Singleton, the authors have modified the original routes and created 12, less arduous, walks highlighting the importance of the Cromford & High Peak Railway (C&HPR) to the region.

Fully opened in 1831, the C&HPR was conceived to connect two canals vital to the region's industry and only joined up with the national network, via the main Manchester line, in 1853. Eventually closing in 1973, Derbyshire District Council (DDC) and the Peak Park Planning Board (PPPB) decided to develop sections of the route into trails for walking, cycling and horse riding. By the mid '70s, the 17 miles between Hurdlow and Cromford had become the High Peak Trail and the 12-mile branch line, which had operated from Parsley Hay to Ashbourne, had become the Tissington Trail.

When Brian originally began researching the first eight walks, he had little knowledge of the history of the C&HPR and no idea of its route north of Hurdlow after the High Peak Trail ended. Fortunately, the historical importance of this unique railway had not been lost to railway enthusiasts who held a treasure trove of written and photographic material, including videos containing archival footage of the railway and the personal reminiscences of railway workers of the time.

More sections of the old line and its spurs continue to be opened up and further expansion and public access is promised. As well as buying up sections of the track bed, the DDC and the PPPB also purchased a number of the original railway buildings – such as the engine house at Middleton Top, the workshops at High Peak Junction and Cromford Wharf and the light railway at Steeple Grange on the old Killer's branch line – which are now manned by enthusiastic volunteers only too ready to pass on their extensive knowledge of the railway and its history. There are also numerous information boards at the most significant points along the line.

The 12 walks in this book aim to bring walkers back to the fascinating history of this amazing railway and the glorious countryside through which it passed on its full journey between the Cromford canal in the south and the Peak Forest Canal in the north and the critical part it played in the region's – and the nation's – industrial story.

Find us on Facebook:

[f] facebook.com/walking the C&HPR

Hindlow Station & Brierlow Lime Works

Two Blokes a Book and a Railway

About The Authors

Brian Bethune was born and grew up in hill country – the Lake District – so it wasn't really surprising that whilst working as a research metallurgist at Manchester University, he chose to make his home in Derbyshire, in the High Peak, where he could indulge his love of walking right from his doorstep. He's also a bit of a railway buff.

Dave Singleton, spent his early career in the Royal Navy and, ironically, he now lives just about as far away from the sea as is possible in Britain. His home near Ashbourne, gateway to Dovedale in the Peak District, nourishes Dave's life-long love of walking, which began in his native Lancashire, and progressed to more serious walks including the Coast to Coast Walk (192 miles St. Bees – Robin Hood's Bay). He likes old railways too.

The two became friends when they met on a charity walk on behalf of "Free Tibet" in the mid '90s and, sharing a passion for walking, they've been putting their boots on together ever since. Not only have Brian and Dave explored every nook and cranny of their own bailiwick of the Peaks but have also tackled the fells of the Lake District and 'done' all 214 'Wainwrights'. Venturing beyond home shores, the two negotiated the classic, 125-mile Haute Route over the French and Swiss Alps – Chamonix to Zermatt – together in 2004.

With over 100 years of walking experience between them, this guide distils everything they know about what makes a great walk.

Brian: "The Peak District, incorporating the southernmost part of the Pennines, is fantastic country for walking, but once you also know something of the history of the place – both early manufacturing, the first canals and some of the earliest railway tracks – and its crucial role in the development of Britain as an industrial superpower, it transforms a great walk into a fascinating history lesson. The Cromford & High Peak Railway played a major role in the region's success so writing a book which brought all that together was a no-brainer."

Brian Bethune & Dave Singleton

Walking Along a Piece of History

The Importance of the Cromford and High Peak Railway

The Industrial Revolution delivered probably the single biggest change to the social order in Britain since the Norman conquest. It was the railways that sent it around the world.

Steam power, the mechanisation of manufacturing and the mass movement of people to new towns to work the machines was to forever change the nature of society and satisfying that relentless beast demanded a whole new way of bringing in raw materials and shipping out finished goods. Initially, water was the obvious solution.

On poor roads, the packhorse and the wagon were expensive, slow and not very efficient. Canals were cheap and quick. When the Duke of Bridgewater built the nation's first canal in 1761 to carry coal from his mines in Worsley to the cotton mills in Manchester – a distance of 10 miles – it meant a single horse could pull 30 tons at a steady speed. At its peak, in the mid-1850s, some 4,250 miles of canals connected all the country's major industrial centres, ports and rivers.

Taking full advantage of the route of the river Erewash, rising in Nottingham and flowing through Derbyshire to join the river Trent at Long Eaton, the Erewash canal was planned to serve the collieries along the Nottinghamshire/Derbyshire border. Its opening in 1779 meant that the whole of the Midlands canal system was now linked with the mighty Trent. By 1794, the Cromford canal extension came up the Derwent Valley to bring coal to Richard Arkwright's mill (the first water-powered cotton spinning mill in the world and now part of the Derwent Valley Mills World Heritage site) at Cromford and then ship the finished goods back out into the Empire.

Further north, the Rochdale and then the Ashton canals coming out of Manchester were extended south down the Goyt valley to connect into the Peak Forest canal at Dukinfield, thus creating a continuous waterway between the mills, coalmines and quarries of the Peak District and the growing industrial regions of south Lancashire, based around Manchester. At the terminus of the Peak Forest canal, the basin at Bugsworth, one of the largest inland ports on the canal system, opened in 1796 and then the Whaley Bridge Basin in 1800. It was here that the Cromford & High Peak Railway began some thirty years later.

Spanning the 33 miles which separated the Cromford canal in the south from the Peak Forest canal in the north was an obvious next move but the terrain – a high, intervening, limestone plateau rising to over 1,000 feet above sea level – meant cutting a new canal was both technically difficult and ruinously expensive. A canal survey in 1810 followed the Derwent north through Bakewell before turning west up the Hope valley through Edale, then, via a 2.75 mile tunnel taking it under the High Peak, to emerge to the north-east of Chapel-en-le-Frith. The estimated cost was prohibitive and so the enterprise was abandoned.

It was the railways which provided the means and the money.

When Richard Trevithick used a steam locomotive to haul goods along a tramway in Wales in 1804, it was the world's first-ever railway journey. In 1825, the C&HPR obtained a warrant from Parliament for a "railway or tramroad" to be propelled by "stationary or locomotive steam engines" – remarkably prescient considering George Stephenson's now world-famous Stockton to Darlington line had only just got going up in Durham and most people believed that steam locomotion was unfeasible. It was not until 1830 that the world's first time-tabled passenger service – running between Liverpool and Manchester – was inaugurated.

Long before locomotive power, however, tramways were already in use, especially in the coalfields of the north east, as horses hauling loads on rails could pull ten tons compared to only one ton on a good road. However, whether horse-drawn, canal or early, low-powered steam locomotion, they all baulked at hills.

Canals went around hills wherever possible, and, where going up (or down) was unavoidable the level changes were negotiated by locks. When Josiah Jessop eventually set about building the C&HPR line and was faced with the mighty task of raising the line from 517ft at Whaley Bridge up to 1266ft at Ladmanlow and then back down to 278 ft at Cromford he had to use inclined planes and static winding engines. It was one of the highest lines ever built in Britain and the 33 miles needed nine inclined planes, all with stationary steam winding engines.

The first part of the C&HPR line – from Cromford Canal Wharf to Hurdlow – opened in 1830. The line used cast-iron, 'fish-bellied' edge rails sitting on stone blocks. Each rail was 4 ft in length and weighed in at 84 lbs each. All told, the original track, including 'doubling' on the inclines and passing loops, needed

100,000 rails. On the inclines, the stationary steam engines drove continuous loops of chain, to which the wagons were attached. This meant over seven miles of chain.

Steam locomotion was still the exception, however, and most tramways, including the C&HPR, continued to rely on horsepower until, in 1833, a steam locomotive named 'Peak', built by Robert Stephenson in Newcastle, was delivered to the line. Gradually, all levels saw the introduction of steam locomotives and, during the 1860s, the line took out a licence to carry passengers in a 'fly' attached to the goods wagons.

As the engines got heavier to cope with the increased loads, the relatively brittle, original cast-iron rails began to break under the pressure, particularly on tight curves. The rigidity and shortness of the rails, resting on stone blocks, meant an uncomfortable, noisy, jolting ride for passengers and these began to be replaced by wrought-iron rails on transverse wooden sleepers.

Although the line had been developed to transport goods between established sites, very quickly new industries, in particular limestone quarries and lime kilns, sprang up along its length and these were to be the primary users during its lifetime.

It wasn't until 1853 that the line joined up with the nation's burgeoning railway network when a one-mile spur, from Cromford Wharf to High Peak Junction South, connected the C&HPR to the Manchester, Buxton, Matlock and Midland Junction Railway. Shortly thereafter, this company took over the whole line. Operating the line continued to be intensely demanding, however, as wagons moving up and down the inclines meant continually changing engines, resulting in highly variable journey times.

Over the next decades, additional connecting spurs continued to expand the line's reach. At the northern end, Whaley Bridge was joined up with the Stockport, Disley and Whaley Bridge lines. The Stockport line was then extended through Chapel-en-le-Frith to reach Buxton in 1864. In 1892, a line south out of Buxton connected into the C&HPR at Hindlow. This led to the Ladmanlow to Shallcross line being abandoned. Various line improvements brought realignment and doubling of the line between Hindlow and Parsley Hay and the bypassing of the Hurdlow incline.

Rivalry between the London North Western Railway (LNWR) – which had owned the C&HPR since 1887 – and the Midlands Railway prompted the LNWR to create a London connection to Buxton by planning a new line from Parsley Hay to Ashbourne (opened 1899) and Uttoxeter. Unhappily, these plans were never fully implemented.

Although open to passengers from the 1860s, the line was dominated by goods traffic, predominantly from the quarries, but road transport was slowly eating into the volumes carried and, from 1952 onwards, the line began to decline. This sad, slow demise of a once-proud and vital railway, intensified during the Beeching cuts of the 60s, finally ended when the Harpur Hill to Hindlow section closed in 1973. Today, only a two-mile section of track, still using the original C&HPR track bed, remains open, carrying minerals from Dowlow quarry.

From its earliest beginnings as the water and then the rail route for raw materials and manufactured goods to and from the industrial powerhouses of Britain in the 18th century, the C&HPR line has been re-invented in the 21st century as one of the most celebrated walking trails in the Peak District National Park. Taking a walk along the line is to take a walk straight through the nation's history and our industrial heritage.

Dowlow Winter 1955

Whaley Bridge Start of Walk 1

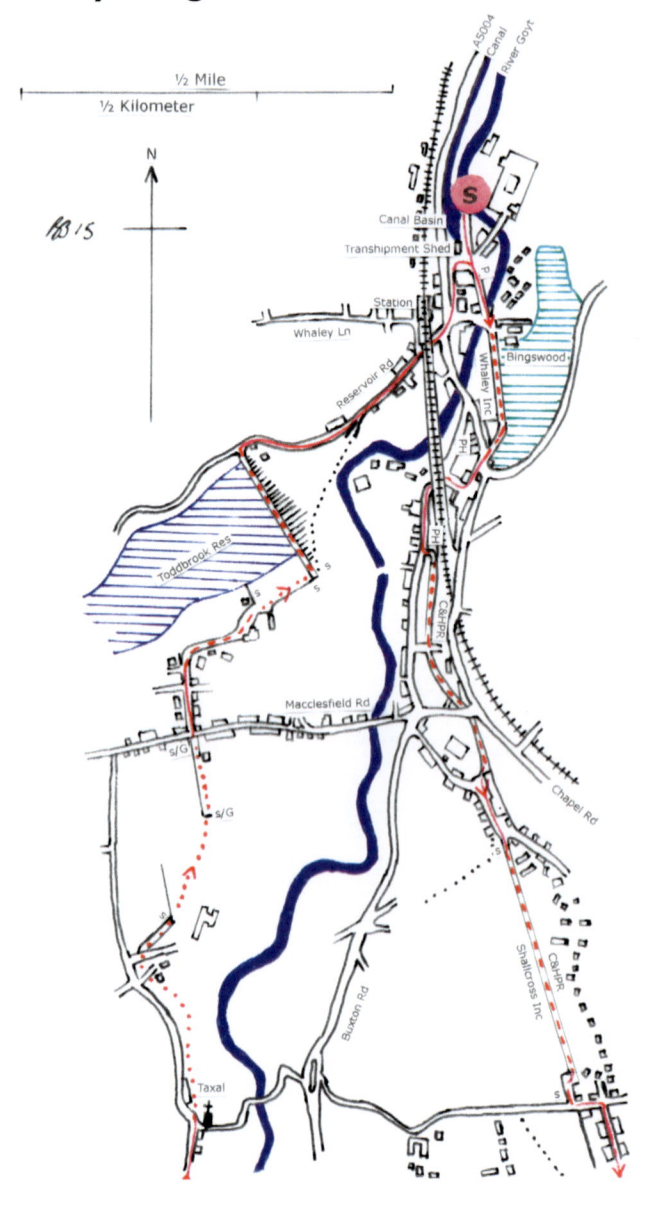

Walk 1 Map

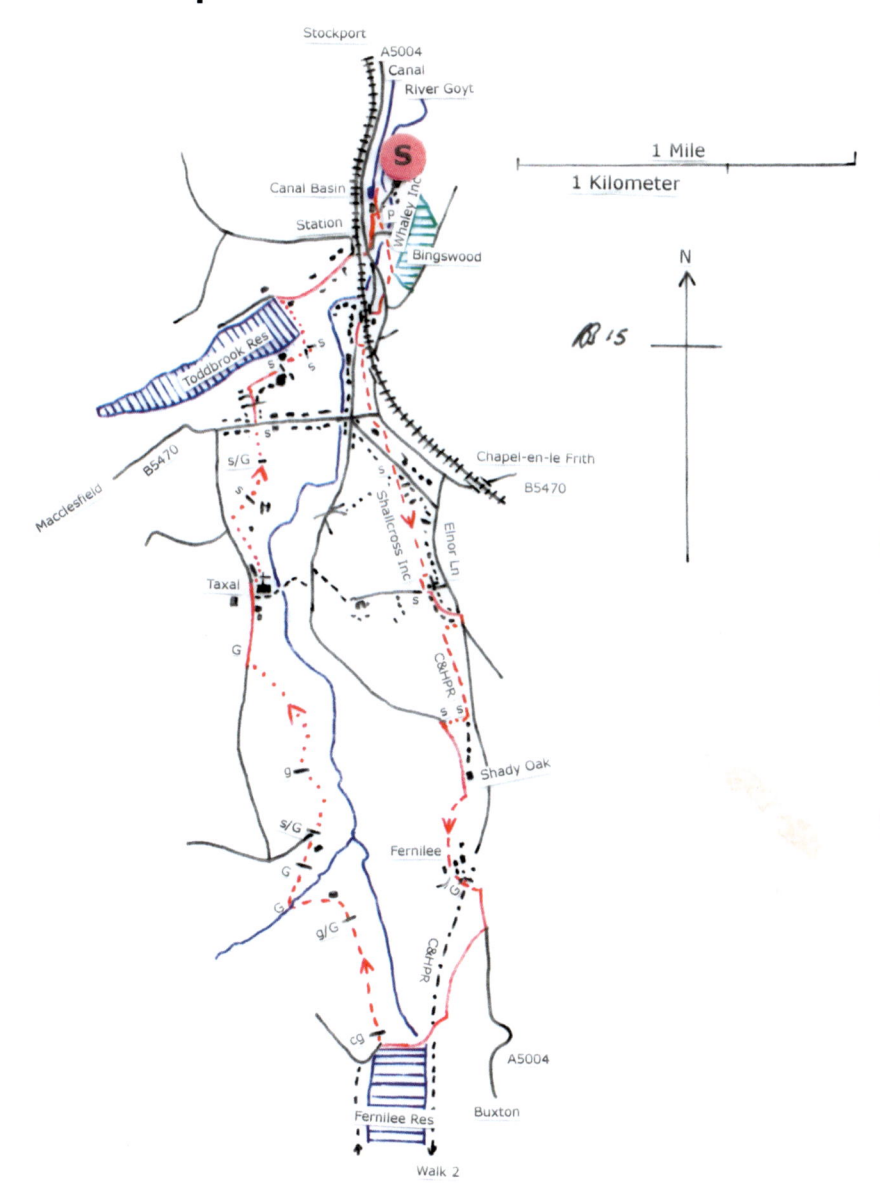

Walk 1 WHALEY BRIDGE – FERNILEE

Route:
Whaley Bridge Canal Basin - Whaley Incline - Shallcross Incline - Fernilee - Fernilee Reservoir - Taxal - Toddbrook Reservoir - Whaley Bridge Canal Basin.
Distance:
6.75 miles (10.9km)
Difficulty:
Leisurely, some field walking. Ascent/Descent 279ft (85m)
Start:
Whaley Bridge Canal Basin. (SK 012 815)
Parking:
There is a car park close to the canal basin but it can quickly fill up during the week. Parking is permitted on the A6 north of the station.

Whaley Bridge Canal Basin

The walk starts from the far end of the canal at its widest point near to the overflow weir. Here the indent in the canal basin edge marks the position of a spur that ran out towards the river Goyt.

At this point canal boats could be run in and be loaded directly from the wagons of the C&HPR, which abutted the spur. Other sidings ran along adjacent to the canal basin and into the main warehouse for transshipment. At a later date the spur was filled in and the line extended over the Goyt to allow coal to be delivered directly to the new boiler house of the Print Works.

Head south along the basin to the far end of the storage warehouse. (Look for red "Transport Trust" plaque on warehouse wall corner with mention of C&HPR 1831)

WHALEY BRIDGE WHARF

Peak Forest Canal wharf & transhipment warehouse (1801), later a terminus of the Cromford & High Peak Railway (1831)

For further information visit: www.transportheritage.com

Continue along the road passing the car park on the left. This is the starting point of the way-marked Shallcross Trail that is followed for the next mile and a quarter.

Cross the river Goyt by a fine original single-track wrought-iron girder bridge with the rails still in place. Note the cast-iron points lever on the far right side. This lever was originally positioned further on and operated the points for the siding into Goyt Mill. Make a small detour L to view the cast-iron mill plate at the entrance to the estate and the adjacent information board.

The Goyt Mill, built in 1865, had the largest single weaving room in England. On the far side of the bridge is Bridge Street, and at this point a branch line into the Goyt Mill turned off left. The Mill was closed in 1976, demolished and replaced by houses.

Cross Bridge Street to reach the foot of the Whaley Incline, indicated by a marker post "Shallcross Trail".

Whaley Incline

Length = 540ft
Incline = 1 in 13.5
Altitude: Bottom = 525ft Top = 590ft Elevation = 40ft
From 1838–1862 the motive power was a 10hp steam powered winch. This was abandoned when mining subsidence damaged the engine house foundations.
From 1862–1952 the motive power was by horse capstan.
Because of the shallow nature of the incline it was always operated using iron chains for hauling.

Whaley Bridge Incline

At the top of the Incline the track bears right to reach the open crossing of Old Road.
Look down to the right to see Whaley's oldest pub, The Shepherds Arms, a name synonymous with the original rural market town before industrialisation made it a favourite with the local coal miners. Directly opposite, the two-storey building was a smithy, which served both the adjacent Gisbourne coal mine and the C&HP railway. Looking up left (Bings Road), the promi-

nent tower is a ventilation shaft for the mine, which was the largest of all the local mines and was open from 1815 to 1911. At this point the seams for this mine are beneath your feet and contour along the hillside in both directions.

Cross the road and continue walking behind the row of terraced houses of Caldene Terrace. Unfortunately the way ahead is now barred as the original track now passes through a private commercial yard.

When first built, this section carried on to the bottom of the Shallcross Incline. However when the Stockport to Buxton line was built in 1863 the C&HPR was realigned to pass under the new railway by a low bridge that had insufficient clearance for the passage of most locomotives. Hence, from this point, the line back down to the canal basin depended mostly on horses for wagon movement right through until its closure in 1952.

Turn R at the way-marked post and drop down to reach Market Street. Turn L and pass under a fine cast iron bridge (No.42) carrying the Buxton – Stockport line over the main road. This bridge, built in 1863, is a listed structure. After passing the Cock Inn proceed L up the enclosed footpath beside the end house. At the top, we return to the track bed of the C&HPR and the main line spur down to the Shallcross sidings.

Up above us we can see the Buxton-Stockport line and on the track side the remains of a loading gauge used to protect the bridge under the main line. Looking back north at this point we would originally have seen two lines dividing, the one on the left climbing to connect onto the main line, while the C&HPR on the right passed right through the low bridge.

Continuing S pass closely behind houses to finally reach the Horwich End cutting. Immediately after going under the road bridge note the mile marker on the right at ground level, 32 miles from Cromford Wharf (opposite the bench). After approx. 80yds the entrance to what was Shallcross Goods Yard is reached, marked by a ground-mounted plaque displaying the C&HPR crest and one of the original cast iron fish-bellied rails.

Horwich End Cutting

This once busy 6-lane siding handled the traffic coming in and out from the surrounding mills and bleach works and the traffic down to the canal basin. Coal was one of the main imports both for the Whaley Bridge gas works (built 1927 and demolished 1963) and for powering the mills. It was over the concrete retaining wall on the right that coal was tipped to directly feed the adjacent retort house. The vertical retorts of the Hoffman design required an extremely tall structure, which was a major landmark in the area for many years.

The sidings and associated warehouse are now occupied by a residential home, Cromford Court. Go past the Court to the foot of the Shallcross Incline and go through the stile to ascend the incline. Near the top the track has been diverted into the adjacent field due to building development on the original track bed. Pass through the final stile to reach Shallcross Road.
(Some time in the future it is hoped to continue the trail directly ahead to reach the true top of the incline...)

Shallcross Incline
Length = 2436 ft
Incline = 1 in 10.5
Altitude: Bottom = 574ft Top = 804ft Elevation = 238ft
From 1838 – 1892 powered by a stationary steam engine

Foot of Shallcross Incline

Turn L along the road and then first R up Shallcross Avenue to the end. Turn R for a short distance and then R again opposite the (wall enclosed) shaft of the original Shallcross cross. Passing between an assortment of garages bear L across a children's playground to return to the Trail through a small wood. Turn L on the trail through a gap in the fence to follow a series of power lines.

Looking back, the wood denotes the position of the engine house atop the incline, while the children's playground on the right marked the position of the feed reservoir.

Go through a metal gate and after approx. 150yds turn R through a wall stile just below Far End Cottages. Cross the field below to a signed stile and back onto the A5004. Turn L and keep to the verge passing the old garage to reach a pavement leading up to the Shady Oak pub. Here take a small detour L to view the track bed in both directions as it passed closely behind the pub. Return to the road and continue L on the pavement.

Ahead the railway originally went under a road bridge but realignment has destroyed the left hand portal. However, the right hand one can be seen under the wall just beyond the millstone marking the boundary of the Peak District National Park.

Prior to this, cross the main road and turn down the road flanked by 2 white metal gate posts and marked by a footpath sign. Looking up to the left, the route of the C&HPR can be seen coming out from the bridge. On reaching the attractive hamlet of Fernilee the lane bends sharp left, and then as it starts to turn right, detour up L for a short way to observe the very tall arched bridge that carried the railway over the access track. Return and carry on round for a short way to meet the farm access track (Folds End Farm), swinging immediately left to pass Fernilee cottage. Go up a walled green lane to reach a metal gate with the track bed crossing in front in both directions. Carry on to the top of the lane and go R on the pavement beside the main road. In approx. 100 yards turn R downhill on the reservoir access road.

This access road was put in in 1932 when work started on Fernilee Dam. It allowed workers and equipment to be brought into the construction site. The descending straight section of road was lined on both sides by a tin-hutted village used by the construction workers.

At the bottom of the straight descent the road bends left and right before coming down to join the track bed again. Look R to see where the track came in from the north. To the south the track bed hugged the cliff running behind the car park as it headed up the Goyt valley.

Cross over the dam and at the far side turn R along a track above the River Goyt providing excellent views back across the valley. The level track passes over a cattle grid before reaching Knipe Farm after 750 yards. Descend with the track to the wooded ravine and cross via a gated stream (Mill Clough) before continuing uphill R to Madscar Farm. Follow the lane up to the left of the farm. At the top of the lane turn R at the sharp bend through a gate onto a field track. Follow the track beside the wall to the point where it drops down to the field. The track bisects the field keeping above the marshy reed area to reach the descending wall. Cross a stream with a gate opposite. Follow the indistinct path, bearing slightly R to join the path coming up from the Hillbridge and Park Wood Nature Reserve. Now angle L from the wall across the rough pasture going NW to a reach a prominent signpost on the edge of Whiteleas Road. Go through the gate to follow the road out into the fenced lane that leads to the village of Taxal. After passing by the church of St James leave the road to go straight on in front of a row of houses on a gravel drive, finally passing the Chimes of Taxal sign. The path then takes in a wooded section before crossing a driveway with large metal gates. Turning R, follow the fence-enclosed path down to reach a wooden stile into open fields. Keep L to miss the boggy ground.

At the bottom of the field turn L through a gateway to follow the path and carry on directly to the houses bordering Macclesfield Road. Cross over into Reddish Lane and follow this to the far end where it bends right to bring Toddbrook reservoir into view. Leave the lane by a stile besides a barn on the left and carry on along the field footpath to reach the stile at the end of the dam.
Cross the dam and at the far end turn R on Reservoir Road down into Whaley Bridge. Cross directly over Market Street and turn L on Canal Street to reach the canal basin and the walk finish.

Whaley Bridge C&HPR under LNWR

Walks 2 & 3 Map

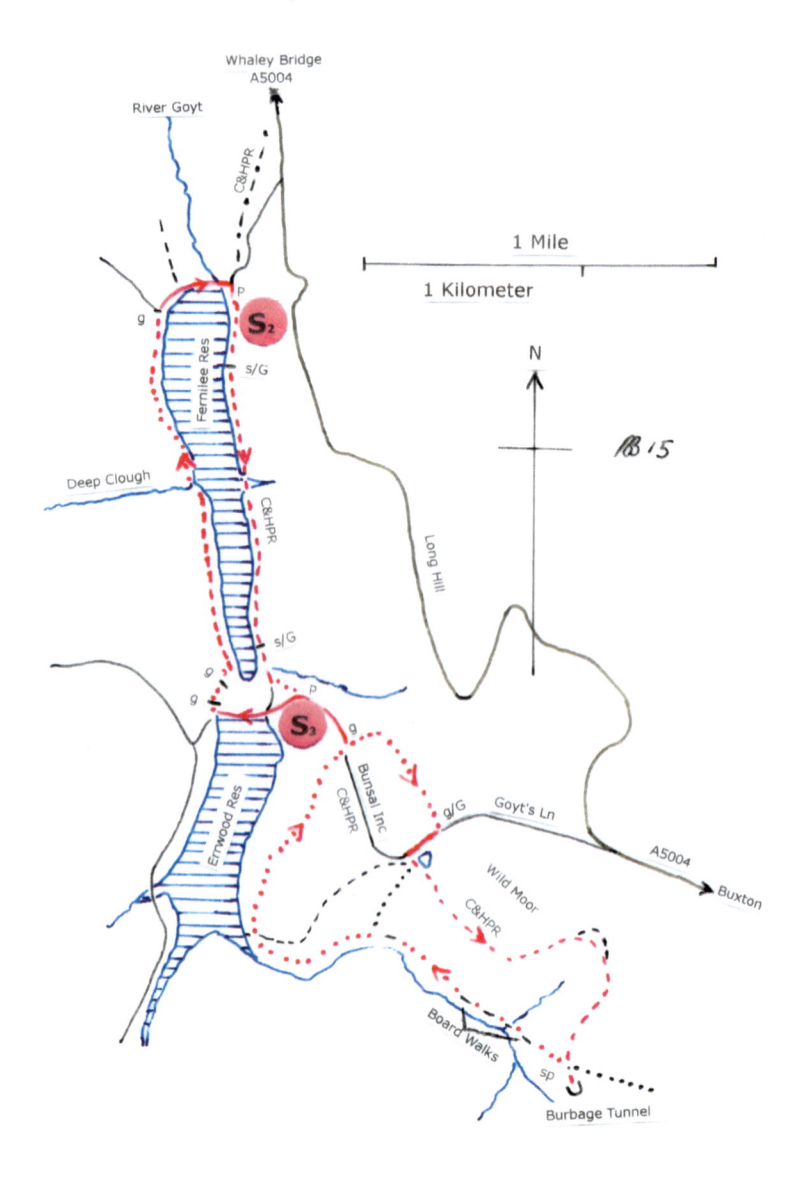

Walk 2 FERNILEE RESERVOIR

Route:
Round Fernilee reservoir
Distance:
2.95 miles (4.75km).
Difficulty:
Easy recreational walk. Ascent/Descent 131ft (40m)
Start:
Fernilee Dam Car Park. (SK 015 777)
Parking:
The car park at the dam of Fernilee Reservoir is reached by the access road that leaves the A5004 Long Hill road, 0.4miles south of the Shady Oak (SK 017 782).

Fernilee Reservoir

From the car park at the eastern side of Fernilee reservoir dam, the route along the side of the reservoir coincides with the track bed of the C&HPR. This part of the route is particularly attractive and is a popular local recreation walk where a circuit of the reservoir makes for a pleasant stroll.

Although this part of the line was abandoned in 1892 the sound of steam returned nearly 40 years later when construction of the reservoir started (1931-1937). The plateau area adjacent to the car park was the hub of the construction site with offices, engine shed and a network of 3ft gauge line to service the site.

Leave the car park going S on the track beside the reservoir wall. Just before the first stile look left to see a track coming down past the ruins of Shawstile farm. This track originally crossed the C&HPR line on its way down to the Fernilee Gunpowder Mill situated in the bottom of the valley.

Gun Powder Works

The mill was originally licensed in 1801 to produce blasting powder for the local mines and quarries. It did however go on to produce powder for munitions during the Boer and 1st World Wars before closing in 1920.

On reaching a wooded section, a shallow cutting is entered.

The wood screened the line from the main factory below. Because of the hazardous nature of such a manufacturing process these sites were remotely located and the storage magazines were some distance from the mill. They were served, in this case, by a network of narrow gauge tramways.

Gun Powder Factory Workers

Continue along the track until the dam of Errwood Reservoir is reached. This is where the foot of the original Bunsal No.1 Incline was situated. Follow the access road up the incline. Where the road bends right, the route of the original incline continues straight on and can be seen behind the fence passing upwards through the under-growth and trees. Turn L off the track to follow the footpath up the grass embankment. Near the top look left over the fence to see the remains of bridge No.57 where an old track passed over the incline.

On reaching the road turn R and follow the road bending L and then R across the top of the dam. At the far end of the dam climb the grass bank and turn R through the gate. Follow the footpath forking R back down to Fernilee Reservoir. Now walk back on the lower of two tracks down the western edge of the reservoir through mixed woodland incorporating several conifer plantations. Enjoy the good views back across the water to our outbound route along the C&HPR track bed. Just over half way along the reservoir the track becomes a footpath and begins to climb gradually away from the shoreline. Eventually it rises more steeply up a boarded, stepped section to meet the higher woodland trail. Here turn R, signed Fernilee, and walk down the track to join the access road signposted 'Hoo Moor'. Turn R on to the lane following it round to reach the edge of the dam. Cross the dam to arrive at the car park.

Bunsal Bottom from Western Bank

Goyt Valley Reservoir Construction

Walk 3   BUNSAL INCLINE - BURBAGE TUNNEL

Route:
Errwood Dam – Bunsal Inclines – Burbage Tunnel – Wild Moor – Errwood Dam.
Distance:
3.85 miles (6.2km)
Difficulty:
Moderate, moorland walking. Ascent/Descent 312ft (95m).
Start:
Errwood Dam Car Park. (SK 018 758)
Parking:
From the road summit of Long Hill (A5004), turn down into the valley at the sign for the Goyt Valley (SK 032 752). Descend Goyt Lane to the small reservoir and then continue on down the incline to park opposite the trees of Bunsal Cob.

The walk starts from the car park at the bottom of the incline.

Bunsal Top Reservoir

On the opposite side of the road is a notice erected by the Stephenson Locomotive Society to commemorate the surfacing of the incline in 1967 to allow motor vehicles access during the building of Errwood Reservoir. (Note the sign's alternative spelling of **Bunsall** *in conflict with the more usual* **Bunsal***).*

Walk up the road to the end of the tree line, and looking down left off the road is the now reed-choked reservoir that fed Bunsal No. 1 incline stationary steam engine. The engine was also positioned on the left hand side of the road. Follow the road up to where footpath signs point in both directions away from the road. Turn off L through the gate onto the open moorlands. Note the adjacent partly filled access bridge under the road. Follow the grass track uphill as it contours right until it finally reaches Goyt Lane at a gate with a 'Peak & Northern' footpath sign No. 250.

Bunsal Incline No.1 Bridge 57

Turn R on the road past the car parks adjacent to the large reservoir that supplied the stationary steam engine at the top of Bunsal No. 2. Make a detour R at the top of the Incline. Here the engine house stood on the left side of the road when looking down.

Bunsal Inclines
No. 1   457yds long at 1:7
No. 2   660yds long at 1:7.5
Opened in 1831 with two stationary steam engines.
The two inclines combined in 1857.
Closed in 1892.

Wild Moor

From the reservoir, follow the track bed on the right SE across the containment embankment. The route now becomes very exposed and remote as it twists and contours round the moorland hills of the aptly named Wild Moor. This was not the place for getting your engine stuck in a snowdrift in the middle of winter! The biggest of the bends which contours round the main clough takes the line through 330° at a radius of 7.6 chains. At this point it can be seen that the track has been doubled with the addition of an outer embankment, possibly constructed from the Burbage tunnel waste material, thus creating a useful passing place. Finally, the way ahead is barred by the blocked northern entrance of Burbage tunnel. Although the outer portal has collapsed, the cutting up to the entrance provides a useful shelter in poor weather for a refreshment stop.

Returning from the face of the tunnel take the signed footpath L ('Wildmoorstone Brook') that drops down the valley on a clear path. Several boardwalks over boggy ground will be encountered on the descent. Beware - these can be extremely slippery in wet weather! After one kilometre you reach a bridge with metal side rails. Without crossing the bridge, take the track ahead signposted 'Errwood / Bunsal'. Continue above the ravine looking down on the reservoir intake creek.

Burbage Tunnel

On rounding a corner note the small lime kiln on the right. Before the building of the reservoir with its accompanying forestation, this valley was one of rural bliss with cultivated fields tended by many farms. Lime was an essential fertilizer and the raw materials for its production, limestone and coal, were within easy carting distance.

A short distance further on is an idyllic viewpoint above the reservoir, complete with bench seat. From the bench cross over the old lane coming in from the right, and take the well defined path to the right of the conifers over a couple of fields with an open view of the reservoir.

Go through a gap in the wood by an oak tree with wall on the right. The grassy path then continues, bisecting some conifer plantations, before climbing gently across open moorland. Head for the old bridge under the road by the way marker – this is where we left the incline at the beginning of the walk.

Turn L on the road, and walk the short distance down to the finish.

Bunsal Lower Reservoir

Walk 4 Map

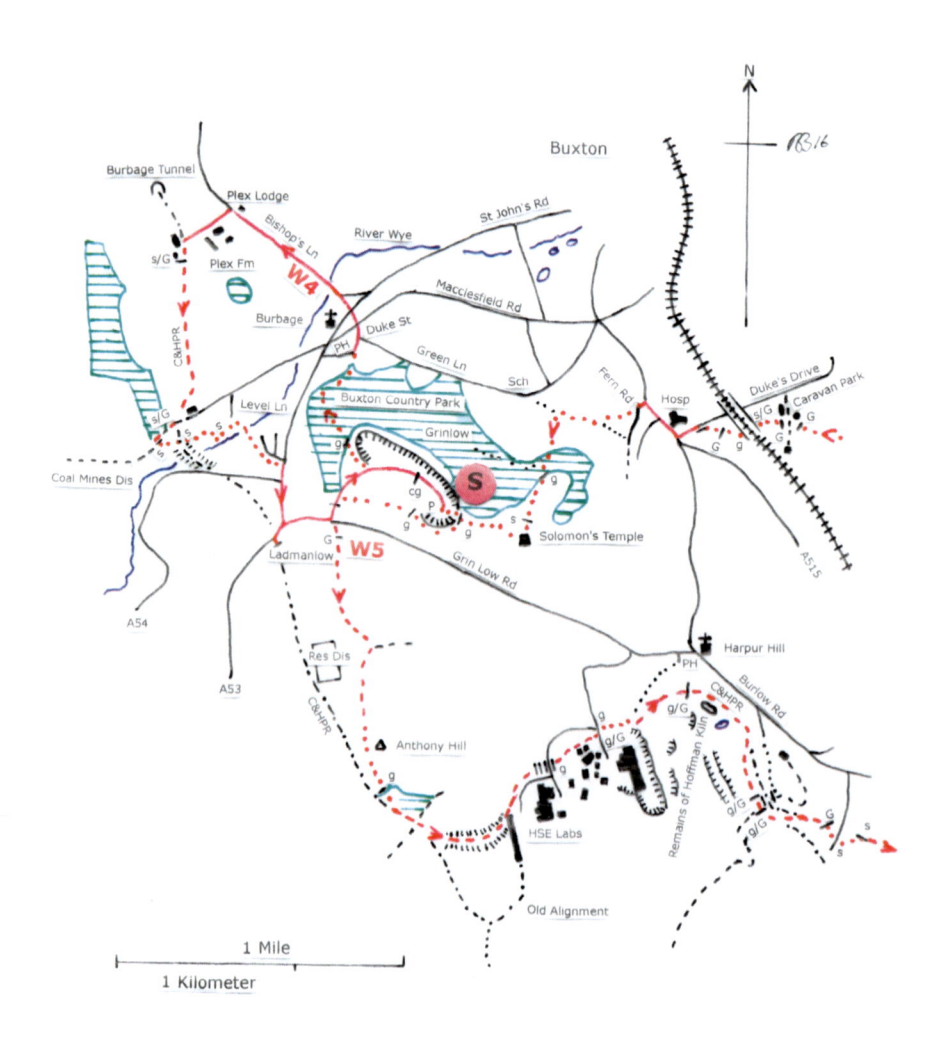

Walk 4   GRINLOW - LADMANLOW

Route:
Grinlow – Burbage – Ladmanlow.
Distance:
4.05 miles (6.5 km)
Difficulty:
Easy track and road walking with two moderately steep footpath descents.
Start:
Grinlow car park. (SK 049 719)
Parking:
The walk starts from the Grinlow car park that has an honesty box. There is a toilet block at the park but take note of the barrier closing times, which vary with the seasons.

The car park is reached from Buxton by following the A53 Leek road from the town to Ladmanlow on the outskirts. Here, where the main road bends right up to the open moorlands, turn L along Grinlow Road. In a short distance turn L again into Grinlow and Buxton Country Park. Follow the access road up and over the cattle grids and down past the quarry campsite to the parking area.

Bridge under Old Macclesfield Road

From the car park walk back up the access road crossing the cattle grid. At the top just after large rocky outcrops where the road bends left, turn off R onto the grass and follow the fence round the edge of the quarry. Descending, reach a second gate signposted to Poole's Cavern and Buxton. Drop down the steps, and take the path L going downhill through the woods, eventually arriving at the wood boundary by a playing field and play area. (The wood has a maze of paths, but if you keep to the most prominent downhill path you shouldn't go far wrong). Finally the path turns down left between the houses to reach Holmfield. Turn R and walk a short distance to the road junction where turning L down Duke Street brings the 'The Duke' pub (latterly 'The Duke of York') into view. Cross directly over the two main roads to the R of the pub into Nursery Lane at the side of Burbage churchyard with its lych gate. Continue down, passing Burbage Band and Burbage Institute Pre-School buildings. At the road junction bear L into Bishops Lane and go straight on and down for a long half mile. On reaching two large stone gateposts straddling the lane adjacent to Plex Lodge, turn L up the access lane to Plex farm. Go up past the farm to meet the track bed of the C&HPR at the top.

To the right lies the southern entrance to Burbage Tunnel, hidden round the corner. A notice warns that this is private with no access. Looking left, the straight track bed can be seen clearly seen running across the moor beneath Burbage Edge.

Turn L on the Trail. Over half a mile later a metal gate is reached with a BT substation to your left. The track is misaligned at this point due to the in-filling of the bridge under the old road. Approximately 50yds up the track opposite a Peak & Northern Footpath sign (no. 188) look L to view the C&HPR issuing forth from the other side of the bridge to cross the valley on an impressive curved embankment.

When the northern section was closed in 1892 the line from the south still remained open to this point to serve the coalmines that existed up on the open moors to the west. The track bed of the branch line can be seen clearly on the far side of the stream. This eventually crossed over by a bridge to enter a narrow defile where the wagons could be filled on both sides by chutes.

Buxton Coal Mines

Two coalfields lie to the west of the town underneath the open moorland and adjacent to Burbage. The early mining of the 17c was of exposed coal seams and transportation was by packhorse teams. In the 19c shaft and drift mining coupled with the use of horse and carts on toll roads accelerated production. With the coming of the C&HPR in 1831 coal extraction reached its peak.

The first drift mine, the Dukes Level, was remarkable in being served by an underground canal system where transport was by boat out to a docking pool. This drift, established in about 1770, extended for 2.5miles under Axe Edge as far as the Staffordshire border. A latter drift mine of 1812, the Goyt New Tunnel, ran for over 3,000yds and utilised a narrow gauge railway for transport.

Mining finally ceased in 1919 when it is estimated 1.8 million tons of coal had been removed. Although not an extensive operation with the underground extraction being dependent on manpower throughout, it was nevertheless crucial in developing the local manufacture of lime from limestone. The limekilns tended to use the poorer quality coal while the best was reserved for domestic use and/or conversion into coke for use in the Sheffield steel industry. Four small beehive ovens are positioned on the hillside adjacent to the mines.

Embankment adjacent to Buxton Coal Mines Sidings

Continue to climb up the track to the first footpath sign and stile L. This steep descent down the bank needs care in wet weather. At the bottom bear L to reach the track bed with the southern portals of the old bridge looking down at you (see photo at beginning of walk). Pass through the metal gate onto the start of the embankment. Immediately turn L to follow a wall and then zigzag down beside a large stone-faced culvert that carries the nascent river Wye under the embankment. Follow the path down to the left of the stream to a residential drive. Here turn R to take the path on the bank of the stream next to the garden fence. Look out for the metal grid on your left from under which water runs from the Dukes Level coalmines, discolouring the Wye red. On reaching the bottom of Level Lane turn down R to cross the Wye. At the white cottage go R onto an enclosed path running along the rear of the new houses. This path takes you to the main road. Turning R, follow the pavement up and continue straight across the road junction with the A54 Congleton / A537 Macclesfield road. Just before the A53 Leek road sign on the L is the position of the gated Ladmanlow level crossing.

Ladmanlow Crossing

The white house was once the railway house serving the adjacent busy marshalling yard which handled coal from the Goyt coal mines and limestone from Grinlow Quarry. Directly opposite, a short section of walled track bed can be followed to a gate where the way ahead towards Harpur Hill can be viewed. Unfortunately there is no access here as this is part of the estate of the Health and Safety Executive Laboratories. If you stand on the embankment on the left side, the curving track bed of the Grinlow quarry branch line can just about be made out. This extensive quarry had its own loco and the junction was controlled by a very prominent semaphore signal.

Turn back along Grinlow road, passing cottages on the right. Return to the car park and walk finish via the Country Park access road.

Ladmanlow

Walk 5 Map

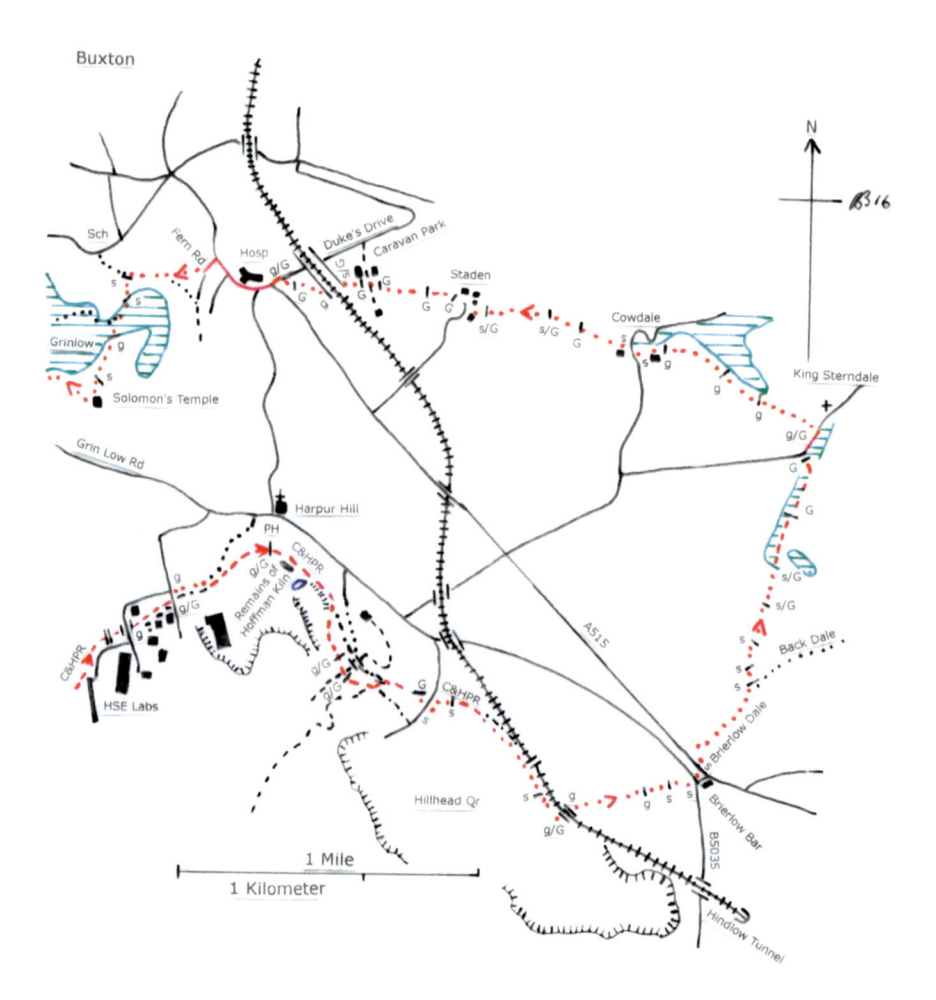

For start of Walk 5, refer to page 32, Walk 4 Map

Walk 5   GRINLOW - BRIERLOW

Route:
Grinlow - Harpur Hill - Hindlow - Brierlow Dale - Cowlow - Staden – Solomon's Temple - Grinlow
Distance:
9.75miles (15.7km)
Difficulty:
Mainly track and field walking but with two ascents: out of Brierlow Dale (100ft <30m>) and up to Solomon's Temple (350ft < 105m>)
Start:
Grinlow Car Park. (SK 049 719)
Parking:
Grinlow Car Park. See Walk 4 for more details…

Exit the car park on the public footpath going E uphill (signposted 'Pooles Cavern / Solomon's Temple'). At the top turn R along a fence-lined track running above the rim of the old quarry. After approx. 250yds pass through a gate and go straight across open pastures heading W for a line of trees adjacent to the Country Park entrance road. Turn L on the road, over a cattle grid and follow down to the Park entrance on Grinlow road.

Old Harpur Cutting

Harpur Hill

Cross directly over and pass through a gate to follow a track down whilst viewing to your right the C&HPR as it proceeds from the Ladmanlow level crossing and then contours across and under the Buxton to Leek road below Axe Edge.

Eventually the walled and wooded disused Stanley Moor reservoir is reached. Just after the corner of the wall where the tracks divides, go to the R and pass round the base of Anthony Hill to come into close proximity of the C&HPR with the numerous experimental rigs of the Health and Safety Executive Laboratories.

At the point where the track continues round the hill, look out for a faint path on the R that runs down to a conifer wood. Follow the broken wall to cross a stream and enter the copse via a gate. Health and Safety notices abound, and occasionally when experiments are been performed red flags fly and access can become restricted. Pass through the wood to reach the track bed, which is now surfaced. Turn L. After 100 yards go straight ahead over the crossroads with associated footpath signs.

On reaching the massive curved embankment note the original alignment of the C&HPR going off to the right through a rock cutting. Its level course can be traced round the valley passing through cuttings and over embankments before reaching the far side of the embankment. The old section was abandoned in 1875 when the embankment was built.

Cross the embankment on the painted marked footpath, curving left.

At the far side note the long concrete tunnel with fence on top, built along the original C&HPR track bed. This was one of the first installations on the site, which was then the 'Safety in Mines Research Establishment'. When coal mining was at its peak at the start of the 20th Century there were some terrible mining disasters related to the explosion of firedamp. This site was chosen because the old track bed provided a long flat straight that allowed a blast tunnel 1,200 ft. in length to be constructed.

Follow the signed track into the cutting to the left of the access road. After passing under two bridges (one new, one old) leave the site through a gate. This is now Old Harpur where the landscape has changed dramatically since the departure of the railway.

Harpur Hill Entrance to RAF Tunnels

To the right there were once sidings that ran in to the tunnels of the RAF ammunition dump and to the ICI lime kilns, which stood in front of the huge quarry face. On the left, sidings served ICI's wagon repair works.

Cross the road and descend the bank to the footpath into fields and follow the footpath along the wall beneath the fenced-in track bed. At the end of the security fence line, scramble up the embankment to rejoin the track bed, heading L with spoil heaps on the right. After approx. 150yds you will meet a newly re-surfaced section of the Trail.

Pass through a gate on a right hand curve and look for the foundations (on top of the old wall) of the of the once giant Hoffman limekiln. This building, reported to be the largest of its type, had a chimney 170 feet high. Built in 1872 to burn lime, the stone was moved in a giant oval to maintain a 24-hour a day production rate. The fire inside burned continuously until 1944. The kiln was demolished in 1951 and the bottom part of the kiln was taken away in April 1980.

Harpur Hill Hoffman Kiln

Continue on the Trail and at the apex of a long right hand bend below a bank of trees, stop to look at the 'new' alignment of 1892 which was situated on the embankment seen below, curving left.

This line was installed in 1892 by LNWR. The original alignment became the branch line serving Hillhead quarry.

After approx. 200yds pass through a pair of well-spaced metal gates. After the second gate proceed on a left hand bend for about 70yds to meet the track coming down from Staker Hill on the right. Turn L here to go downhill to join the embankment via a ladder stile by a gate. Go R along the embankment through a cutting. The way ahead is then interrupted because the bridge over the access road into Hillhead quarry has been removed. Take the footpath R through a metal gate to cross the road before climbing back L up a field to rejoin the track. Shortly, as Hindlow Junction is approached, the footpath climbs up the embankment on the right, to continue to the R of a boundary wall through rough pastures.

In a short distance a large brick access bridge provides a good view of the now single working track to the quarries. Do not cross this bridge; rather proceed forward to reach a stile to leave the fields and go down into an area of abandoned quarrying with a rusty tin roof hut on the bank opposite. The fenced path first drops down beside the railway embankment before climbing up to pass left under the railway line.

Limestone Train from Dowlow

The walk now leaves the C&HPR to return to Buxton. Cross the fields passing over two stiles to reach the corner at the road junction at Brierlow Bar. Cross the Harpur Hill road and the grass island before carefully negotiating the busy A515. Look out for a signed stile to the left of the entrance track to Brierlow Bar Farm. This is the start of Brierlow Dale. Follow the descending track for approx. 500yds until you meet a stile on the left before a central wall stile leading into Back Dale. Go L over the stile and follow a clear path up the dale side to enter fields at the top. Bear R across three fields to reach the corner of a wood. Now follow the track down the edge of the trees to where the track turns left to meet the King Sterndale road. Turn R for a short distance before turning L into fields, signposted by metal gates. Carry on across fields passing by Kid Tor, and arriving in Cowdale to the right of Highcliffe Farm. Bear R across the road to pass via a squeeze stile through a small walled copse and out into open fields. Angle slightly R across two fields and pass close to a disused quarry on your right. On entering the next field aim slightly L to head directly toward the hamlet of Staden.

Here continue ahead on a track passing round to the right of Staden Low to gain a fine panoramic view of Buxton. Drop down the track to cross directly behind farm buildings and continue through a gate to follow the 'Midshires Way' towards the viaduct, above a caravan park. The footpath goes under the top arch and provides impressive views down the length of its 13 arches spanning Dukes Drive. Drop down the track to the road. Turn L and, on reaching the main road, cross over the Drive and follow the pavement R up towards Buxton.

With due caution, cross the main road at a convenient place and then take the second road left 'Fern Road'. In a short way bear R across the grass, following the edge of the trees and head for the far corner to join a walled footpath. At the first entrance into the playing fields on the left cross over towards the wooded hillside of Grinlow. Approximately half way along the playing fields, find the footpath up through the woods, and where it divides go L until open land is reached. Continue on up to the very top and Solomon's Temple.

This folly, a Grade II Listed Building, was originally built in 1896 by public subscription to provide local employment. It is thought that the name Solomon's Temple comes from the name of a local resident, Mr Solomon Mycock of Buxton, who used to rent land up here for farming in the early 1800s. It's worth climbing up inside to enjoy wide ranging views of the surrounding countryside.

On leaving the Temple turn W over the open top, cratered by limestone mining and burning. Keeping to open land, ignore two access gates until you reach steps leading up to the edge of the quarry. Go through a gate and turn L. After a short distance bending right, turn R to go downhill to the car park and the end of the walk.

Solomon's Temple

Walk 6 Map

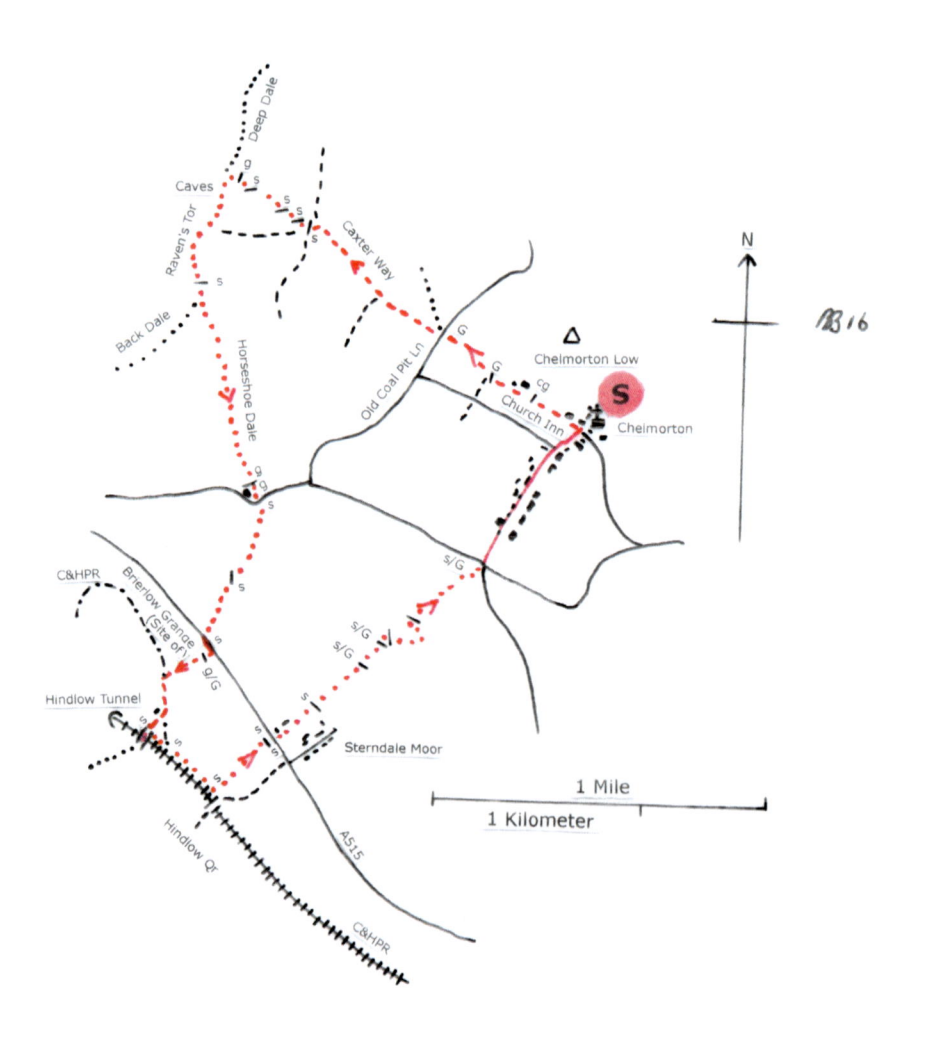

Walk 6   CHELMORTON – HINDLOW

Route:
Chelmorton – Deep Dale - Horseshoe Dale - Brierlow Grange - Hindlow – Sterndale Moor - Chelmorton.
Distance:
5.28 miles (8.5km)
Difficulty:
Moderate. Involves track, field and dales walking. The 150ft (45m) descent into Deepdale is very slippery in the wet and needs care.
Start:
Chelmorton Church. (SK 115 703)
Parking:
At the top end of Chelmorton main street there is good on-road parking next to the church.

Chelmorton with Dowlow and Hindlow Quarries in the Distance

Walk down the main street away from St. John the Baptist's church (note the unusual weather vane, reflecting the saint's time in the wilderness). Pass the Church Inn before turning R on a sign posted track opposite Church Lane. In a short time you reach Shepley farm on the right and after 250 yards the track bends right and left before meeting the A5270. This is 'Old Coalpit Lane', one of many ancient ways connecting the coal mines of Buxton to the surrounding villages, in this case Taddington. Cross the road, taking the footpath on the left (Caxter way Lane) signposted 'Midshires Way'. Go down the track for approx. 900yds and take the second lane on the left. After a short distance go R over a stile, sign-posted 'Midshires Way'. Make your way diagonally over field stiles to reach the edge of Deepdale and Derbyshire Wild Life Trust's Nature Reserve. The way down is steep, so take care on the limestone outcrops as these are particularly slippery in the wet. Near the bottom, the footpath zigzags past a small cave. A few yards down from here turn L and go gradually uphill to reach the mouth of a much larger cave after 50yds.

This is Thirst Hole Cave, extending into the limestone for about 300ft (90m). When excavated by Micah Salt in the late 19c. the cave yielded Romano or Romano-British finds including brooches and manicure and hairdressing items, some of which can be seen in Buxton Museum. Also, outside the entrance at the bottom of the slope were found several burials. A recent review of the finds suggests this was the base for a Romano-British metal working industry, rather than a dwelling.

From here follow the footpath L up the dale as it meanders through the trees above the valley bottom. After passing under high limestone cliffs the footpath emerges to reach the entrance notice board of the Deepdale and Topley Pike SSSI. With scree on the left and a boundary wall on your right, fork L to enter the grassy surface of Horseshoe Dale (Priest's Way). After approx. 850yds go past the entrance to Bullhay Dale on your left, clearly marked as 'Private'! Soon after, pass through gates to the left of farm buildings to meet the road again (Old Coal Pit Lane). Cross the road, bearing L. Look for a hidden stile in the roadside trees. The route now goes diagonally right across this broad dale to climb up to the wall on the skyline. Follow the wall L to a stile in the corner. From this stile, go straight across the field to the trees that border the main road (A515). The stile in the wall is just to the right of a red gas pipeline information plate. Climb up the bank to the road edge and cross the road with care before going L to pass through a lay-by. In a short distance turn R up the drive of what was the lane to Brierlow Grange, now sadly demolished. Follow the track up to the junction with the C&HPR track bed.

To the right the original alignment made a dramatic curving contour round Brier Low before passing over what is now the northern entrance to Hindlow tunnel. The quarry has swallowed most of the route and the way right is barred to access.

Hindlow Tunnel

Turn L and proceed down a typical straight walled section of track bed until the way forward is blocked. Here, turn R to pass by a modern agricultural building before reaching a stone access bridge over the new line. Looking down the line from the bridge the entrance to Hindlow tunnel is visible at the end of a limestone cutting.

When this line was being built in 1891 the cutting proved difficult to dig because of the hardness of the limestone. After the contractors had successfully negotiated increased funding to compensate for the additional work involved, the contractors came across a vein of lead ore for which they obtained mining rights. As can be expected, LNWR asked for some of its money back!

Looking to the south the old alignment that has just been traversed can be seen on a curving embankment crossing an access bridge before it was destroyed by the new alignment.

Access Bridge Old Alignment

During the first half of the 20c this was an extremely busy section of line as the quarries expanded. Up ahead on the right was the well known Briggs siding, served on the left by the Briggs signal box. Although not that obvious on the ground, the OS map clearly shows that the old alignment contained a turning triangle on the right side. Apparently the early wagons had doors at one end, which required them to be facing uphill when negotiating the inclines. Since this is near the summit of the C&HPR, 1280ft (390m), it was a good point to reverse the wagons as it's down hill all the way in both directions.

Briggs Sidings

Go back to the start of the bridge, and take the stile on the right into the field. Follow the footpath to cross over the shallow embankment of the old line. Carry on beside the track boundary wall to approach the quarry access bridge. Here, at the corner of the field, a sign to Chelmorton indicates the footpath turning 90° left to accompany the wall to the trees in the distance. On approaching Sterndale Moor bear R to a fence stile before passing through a small copse adjacent to the A515. Cross directly over the road to find an enclosed footpath up between the houses. On reaching an open area with playing fields follow the wall on the left to a wall stile at the top. From here the next stile is situated diagonally R across, next to a gate halfway down the wall boundary. In crossing the field look for the spire of Chelmorton church appearing directly ahead in the distance. Cross over the stile and go down the track to another stile to the right of a gate. Bear R to a wooden fence stile and descend to the bottom of a dry dale. Turn briefly R before turning back L up the hill to reach a stile at the end of a line of trees. From here head 45° R up and over the lower flank of Nether Low. Go down the descending fields, which are divided by broken walls making the stiles difficult to locate.

Finally exit at a wall stile on the left of the gate opposite the main street into Chelmorton. All that is left now is to stroll back through this tranquil village to the starting point at the church.

Chelmorton

Chelmorton is Derbyshire's highest village, and is claimed to be second highest in England after Flash, just over the border in Staffordshire. Chelmorton is a classic farming village on a limestone plateau at an altitude of 1200ft (366m), positioned beneath the Low of its own name, 1464ft (446m). Chelmorton Low has traces of ancient barrows on its summit. It's well worth the walk up from the gate at the end of the road; the views from its summit on a clear day are spectacular. Just to the right of the entrance to the Low is a spring with the wonderful name of Illy-Willy-Water. In ancient times this was the main source of water for the village and was most likely the reason for Chelmorton's establishment and growth.

Behind the houses on both sides of the street are long narrow walled fields preserving the old medieval cultivation strips.

Chelmorton Church

St John the Baptist is England's highest parish church. Earliest parts of the church are Norman and the low gritstone tower with its little cap of a spire is Gothic. The stone vaulted porch contains a gallery of ancient sculpture and sepulchar slabs. The floor is laid with more of these, about a dozen of them, carved with crosses, coffins, swords and shields. The old village cross stands in the church yard.

Walk 7 Map

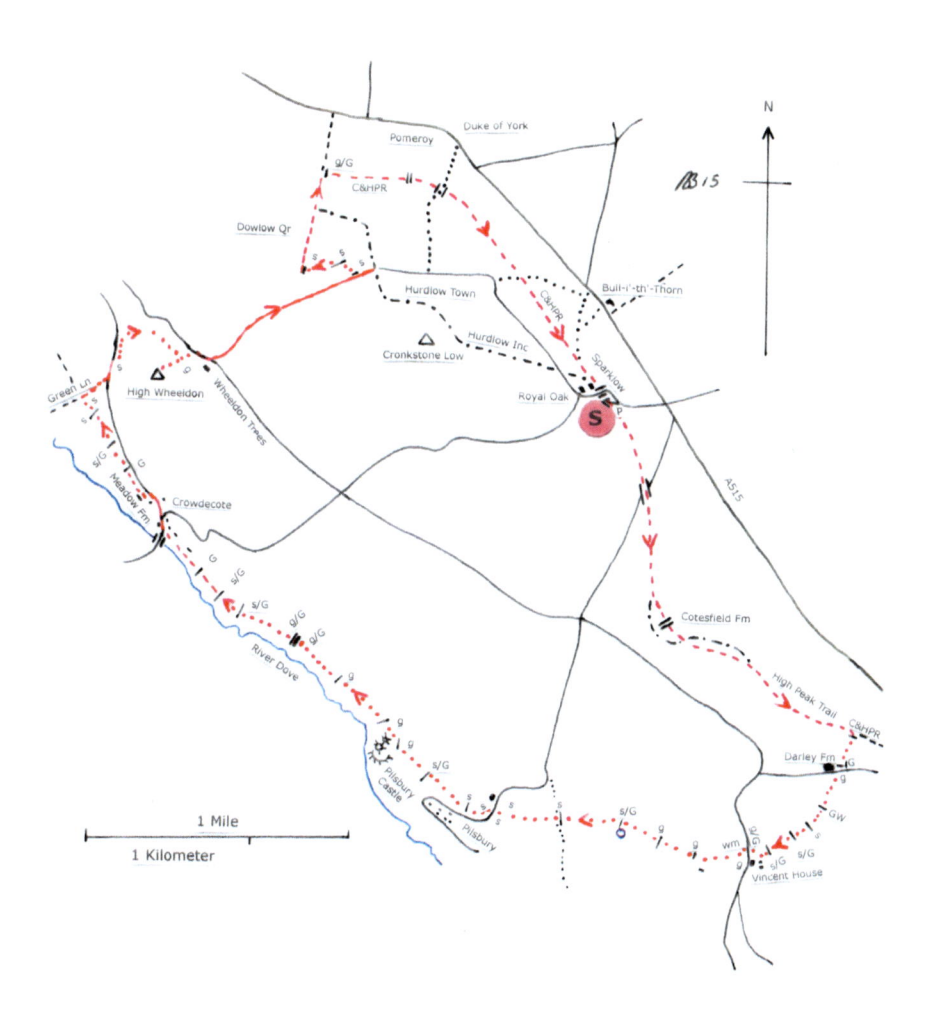

Walk 7   HURDLOW – PARSLEY HAY

Route:
Hurdlow – Parsley Hay – Pilsbury Castle – Crowdecote – High Wheeldon – Hurdlow Town – Hurdlow station.
Distance:
9.6 miles (15.5km)
Difficulty:
Moderate with trail and field walking. Ascent from Green Lane to Wheeldon Trees 262ft (80m), plus another 230ft (70m) to the top of High Wheeldon (optional).
Start:
Car park Hurdlow station ('Sparklow' on OS map SK 128 659)
Parking:
There is ample pay and display parking at the Hurdlow station car park, which includes picnic tables and a brick shelter. Accessed from the A515 Buxton – Ashbourne road, 0.4mi (0.6km) south of the Bull-i'-th-Thorn Hotel, 1.75mi (2.8km) north of Parsley Hay.

Leave the car park taking the High Peak Trail in a southerly direction. After 750yds the trail passes over a minor road.

Further on, as the track begins to bend left round the mixed/conifer wood that surrounds Cotesfield farm, the route becomes part of the new alignment of 1894. The original track carried straight on at this point before making a right angle bend left to cross over the present trail. Its route can be clearly seen on the left as it comes back into alignment.

After going under a bridge, the trail then curves gently right and left before Parsley Hay comes into sight. However, this walk turns off right a quarter of a mile before the station on the signed footpath down to Darley farm. Drop down the steps to enter the field by a stile, then go down to the right of the wall before passing through the farmyard. Cross straight over the road back into fields. Carry straight on up to the left of the boundary wall following the stiles over the hill. On the far side the path becomes a track as it drops down to Vincent House Farm. This area is well sign-posted to prevent straying from the right of way at this working farm! On reaching the farmyard proceed right and left round the farm buildings before crossing the road. It's then up the steps to enter fields where the route is marked with way markers, up and over bearing slightly left. Drop downhill to reach a double-gated stile near a new barn at the field corner. The route now goes up the fields to the right of the power lines. At the second stile the path passes to the right of a large pond that is curiously divided into four by partly submerged walls.

Climbing Hurdlow Bank

From here the path bears slightly left to the next stile where a path running north-south is crossed. The way ahead is now towards a small agricultural building which is passed on the left after crossing the minor road to Pilsbury. The footpath is signed 'Crowdecote' and crosses fields running along the eastern edge above the river Dove. On a clear day it's worth stopping to look back south for fine views of Wetton and Ecton Hills, whilst ahead Chrome and Parkhouse hills are majestic. Continue along the edge left of a boundary wall and look ahead for a signpost in the middle of a field. At the next stile Pilsbury Castle appears below. Follow the path down to where an information board includes a plan of its layout.

Pilsbury Castle

Pilsbury Castle

A scheduled ancient monument, this motte-and-bailey castle was built utilising the natural defences of a limestone reef knoll positioned on a promontory overlooking the river Dove. The date of building is unknown but is likely to be after the Norman conquest of 1066. It was strategically placed to control the local population and trade. Being made of wood, nothing remains of the watchtower and protective palisade or the inner buildings that were used by the garrison. All that remains of man's endeavour are the ditches and banks that now blend with the natural features.

Drop down the path from the rear of the castle and continue NW beside the Dove through fields to Bridge End Farm. Follow this track up to the village of Crowdecote where we reach the road coming in left from Longnor. Continue on past the Pack Horse Inn and at the road junction fork L with 'Two Castles Cottages' on the right. In a short distance turn L on the access road to Meadow Farm (signposted 'Public Footpath to Glutton Bridge'). Pass through the farmyard and follow the track through the fields. On leaving the track continue across two fields to reach Green Lane. Turn R and walk up to join the road and continue uphill to Aldery Cliff on the left and High Wheeldon on the right. Take the stile by the gate on the right at the National Trust sign for High Wheeldon. Follow the footpath up to the right of the wall as it contours up and round towards the col and its northern entrance gate. On a clear day it's well worth climbing up High Wheeldon for the views. The footpath slants up right to the summit trig point (No.S4154), with its memorial plaque.

After summiting, descend back to the gate and turn L to cross the shallow depression before climbing up to reach the road adjacent to Wheeldon Trees Farm Holiday Cottages. Cross over and take the minor road forking L (National Cycle Network route 68). Stay on this quiet high-level route as it climbs over to Hurdlow town.

From the apex of the road there is a fine view of the original alignment as it crosses above the town on an impressive limestone faced embankment, which includes an arched field access bridge. As the track swept round the base of the hill, it reached the top of the Hurdlow incline, where a stationary steam engine stood at the side of the track. The incline was abandoned in 1894 when the new alignment was established.

Walk down to view the track bed in both directions. Retrace your steps a short distance up the road to take the first field stile on the right. Cross the field, go over the stile and turn 90° left to follow the wall for 200yds before going through a squeeze stile onto the cycle track. Turn R and walk up past the southern edge of the massive Dowlow Quarry. On the descent note the line of trees on the right, which mark the continuation of the original alignment. Further down, the entrance and start of the High Peak Trail is reached. Proceed R along the trail on the final stretch of the walk.

The line at this point has a gradient of 1:60 down from the summit at Hindlow so traffic down to Hurdlow could speed along, while that climbing up to the summit would have a bit of a slog and would often be double-headed for the arduous climb. The distance back to Hurdlow station is now 1.5mls (2.5km) and after an initial right curve is a straight run. In the first section the trail passes under two arched brick bridges, the second of which gives access up across a field to the bus stop at Pomeroy. The final straight section passes over three field connector bridges. On approaching Hurdlow station note the power lines coming down from the right, these are positioned on the original Hurdlow incline. When in operation between 1831 and 1894 this area would be busy with trucks being tied on and off the continuous chain of the inclined plane and engines coming and going. Once the new line was established, Hurdlow became very much a rural station handling milk and livestock. However once a year it came to life with the arrival of special trains bringing race goers to Flagg point-to-point races.

After the final (3rd) bridge into Hurdlow, the station house and brick platform with gritstone edging can still be seen on the right. Beyond the bridge stood cattle pens with an access road, which now leads to the Royal Oak Pub and well-earned liquid refreshments!

Hurdlow Town Station

Hurdlow Incline
Length = 2,550ft
Gradient = 1 in 16
Altitude: Top = 1,264ft Bottom = 1,116ft Elevation = 148ft
The winding engine and incline was in operation between 1831 and 1894.

Walk 8 Map

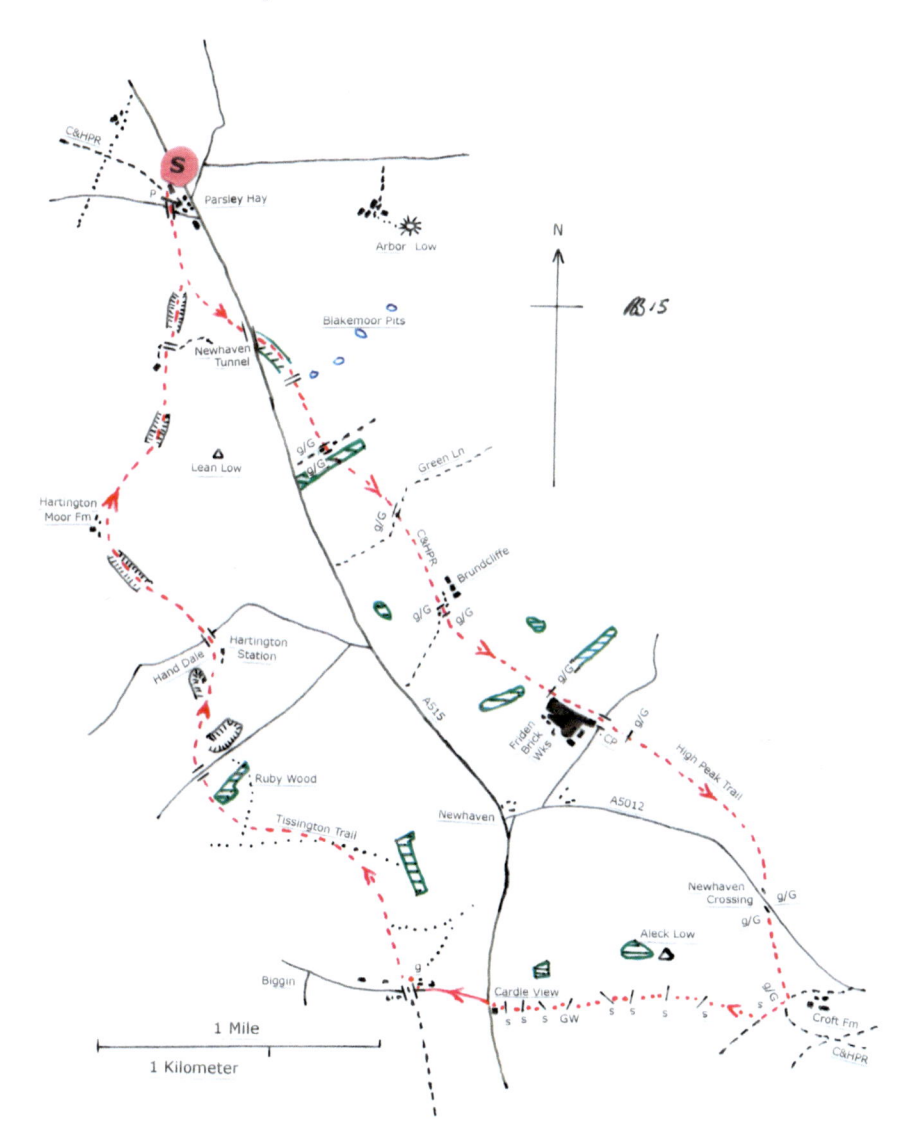

Walk 8   PARSLEY HAY – NEWHAVEN CROSSING

Route:
Parsley Hay – Friden – Newhaven Crossing - Biggin – Tissington Trail – Hartington Station – Parsley Hay.
Distance:
8.25mls (13.27km)
Difficulty:
Easy trail walking with just 1 mile of field walking.
Start:
Parsley Hay station car park. (SK 146 637)
Parking:
Pay and Display at the Parsley Hay station car park.
Facilities available include picnic tables, toilets and a shop.

Leave the Information Centre on the Trail going S, soon to pass over a road bridge where the new station stood.

Parsley Hay Junction

The view south is dominated by the giant cutting that was dug during the construction of the Ashbourne rail link of 1899, and which is now the Tiss-

ington Trail. This development turned Parsley Hay from a quiet rural stop into an important junction with storage sidings for the busy C&HP Railway's heavy freight traffic along with its new main line passenger service from Ashbourne.

Parsley Hay
When built, the C&HPR did one of its little excursions north-east at this point and the station consisted of a short spur that ran out towards the cottages at the back of the car park. When developed at the end of the 19c. realignment turned this area into an extensive goods yard with sidings and a passing loop. The new passenger station was built south of the road bridge on an embankment and access to both platforms was by way of steps up from the road.

After 400yds at the trail junction, take the L fork, which is a continuation of the 'High Peak Trail'. For the next 16.5 miles until its end at Cromford Wharf the trail follows the original 1831 single track that remained unaltered by deviations throughout its life. The right fork is the start of the Tissington Trail running down to Ashbourne 13 miles away. After entering a cutting you reach the short Newhaven Tunnel (153ft, 46m). This goes under the A515.

Newhaven Tunnel

Newhaven Tunnel C&HPR Badge

On the northern portal the carved plaque is of the company's emblem and its motto 'Divina Palladias Arte'. Above it is the name of the railways engineer Josias Jessop while beneath is that of the company's secretary, William Brittlebank. Note the carved stone plaque on the southern portal with a wagon and a reminder this is is the 'Cromford and Highpeak Railway 1825'. The letters at the corners, 'P.H. & Co.' refer to the contractor for this section, Hargreaves & Co.

At the end of the cutting on the right after going under an access bridge, you will see the remains of a signal. Although not obvious on the ground the OS map shows that the line is crossed at this point by a series of sand pits, the Blakemoor pits. These were once connected to the refractory brick works at Friden by their own narrow gauge railway. The Trail is intercepted by a gated farm access lane before bending left and passing through Blakemoor plantation. After another short straight, the trail curves right before crossing Green Lane (signposted left to 'Middleton-by-Youlgreave' and right to the 'A515'). After another straight 500yds Brundcliffe Farm is encountered and soon after the track bends left and the chimneys of Friden Brickworks come into view. When you arrive at this busy factory, look for a series of information boards along its boundary wall describing its history and development. After crossing over the road bridge there is a car park on the right where Friden station and siding once stood. On the adjacent embankment, edging blocks with rails can be seen, the last visible connection with this once busy rail halt and sidings. Note the two 'L&NWR' boundary posts just before the picnic tables, which provide a convenient refreshment stop if desired.

Friden

Although originally just a siding and a goods shed, the commercial success of the brickworks led to its development and in 1895 L&NWR built a new station on the other side of Youlgreave road. This was the furthest south main line engines could venture before running into difficulties with the tight bends. This meant that there was considerable shunting activity here, even though the siding facilities were limited.

Friden Brickworks

The development of the brick works in this area occurred because of the existence of deposits of high purity silica sand and high silica rock known as ganister. The ganister deposits occur because of volcanic activity in this area. Subsequent weathering led to the formation of sands that were deposited into potholes in the limestone strata. It is thought that the clay and sands were laid down in pre-glacial times when river water swirled through large holes down to subterranean levels.

It was in 1892 that John West took out a lease on 4.75 acres of land containing sand pits at Friden and started the manufacture of bricks and fire clay. Latter with an expanding factory and new technology he specialised in refractory bricks under the name of the Derbyshire Silica Firebrick Co. Ltd. This expansion necessitated the sourcing of more local pits of sand and ganister. Transportation back to the factory was first by horse and cart and later with a network of narrow gauge railways. The latter expanded to 15 locomotives operating on 8 miles of track.

The C&HPR played major role in this success. In the early days before reservoirs were constructed it was responsible for supplying the vital water supplies by tanker. It then provided the initial transport of goods, which were then dispatched to all corners of the world.

Today the raw materials are sourced abroad and the continued success of the company lies in its skill in producing complex shapes in specialised refractories that can stand high temperatures and aggressive atmospheres.

From here keep straight on until the next turn right brings the distinctive trees of Minninglow Hill into view on the distant horizon. This next straight takes you to the Newhaven - Via Gellia road (A5012) (Newhaven Crossing). When the railway was operational this was a gated level crossing with an attached gatekeepers house.

Cross the road to continue on the Trail, and after approximately 600yds look for a public footpath sign on the right to 'Biggin' at the point where the Trail is joined by a lane coming up from Croft Farm Holiday Cottages (Upperhouse Farm on the OS). Leave the High Peak Trail at this point to turn R up the farm track, accompanied by a hedge on the right. In about 200yds go R through the hedge via a signed stile into fields. Bearing up L and away from the hedge, the path passes diagonally over the shoulder of Aleck Low. Cross over eight fields by clearly marked stiles and gateways, eventually dropping down to 'Cardle View' on the A515. Cross over the road to continue down the tarmac footpath at the side of the road to Biggin. On reaching the bridge over the road turn R through the gate to gain access to the track bed of the Tissington Trail.

The big change in railway design in the 68 years since the building of the C&HPR will become immediately noticeable. This line proceeds through the undulating landscape by a series of long sweeping curves over numerous embankments and cuttings.

After passing over the first embankment the line makes a leisurely turn left under an access bridge with Horseshoe Plantation up on the right. After another embankment Ruby Wood is gained on the right. This was opened in 1991 to commemorate 40 years existence of the Peak District National Park. The picnic tables are usefully positioned to be sheltered by the wood and provide a convenient refreshment stop. A little further on the track is crossed by a brick and steel girder bridge taking a minor road down into Hartington. Bending right through a shallow cutting a large limestone quarry is seen on the right. More quarries on both sides of the track are encountered before Hartington station is reached. Here there is a restored signal box, picnic tables and a toilet block. If the weather is inclement, shelter can be had in the linesman's hut at the rear of the car park.
Note again the L&NWR.Co. boundary posts.

Hartington

Hartington like Tissington was marketed very much as a tourist station offering easy access to the nearby scenic beauty of Dove Dale. To this end L&NWR built a substantial station at Hartington with platforms on both sides having booking facilities, Ladies and Gents toilets, a Ladies waiting room and a general waiting room.

However, the nearby limestone quarries meant it was also a busy commercial station, with a goods yard, shed and signal box.

The passenger service was withdrawn in 1954 and the line was closed 1967.

Hartington Signal Box

On leaving the station the three-arched viaduct spanning Hand Dale is crossed. Continue on L and R through cuttings to pass Hartington Moor Farm. After another embankment the trail bends left passing a lineman's hut that has been turned into a useful shelter. Continue ahead passing the disused Parsley Hay silica sand pits to go under their access bridge.

Finally, the last and largest cutting is negotiated, 900ft (275m) long with a maximum wall height of 80ft (24m). On emerging, the High Peak Trail is rejoined shortly before your arrive at Parsley Hay and the end of the walk.

Walk 9 Map

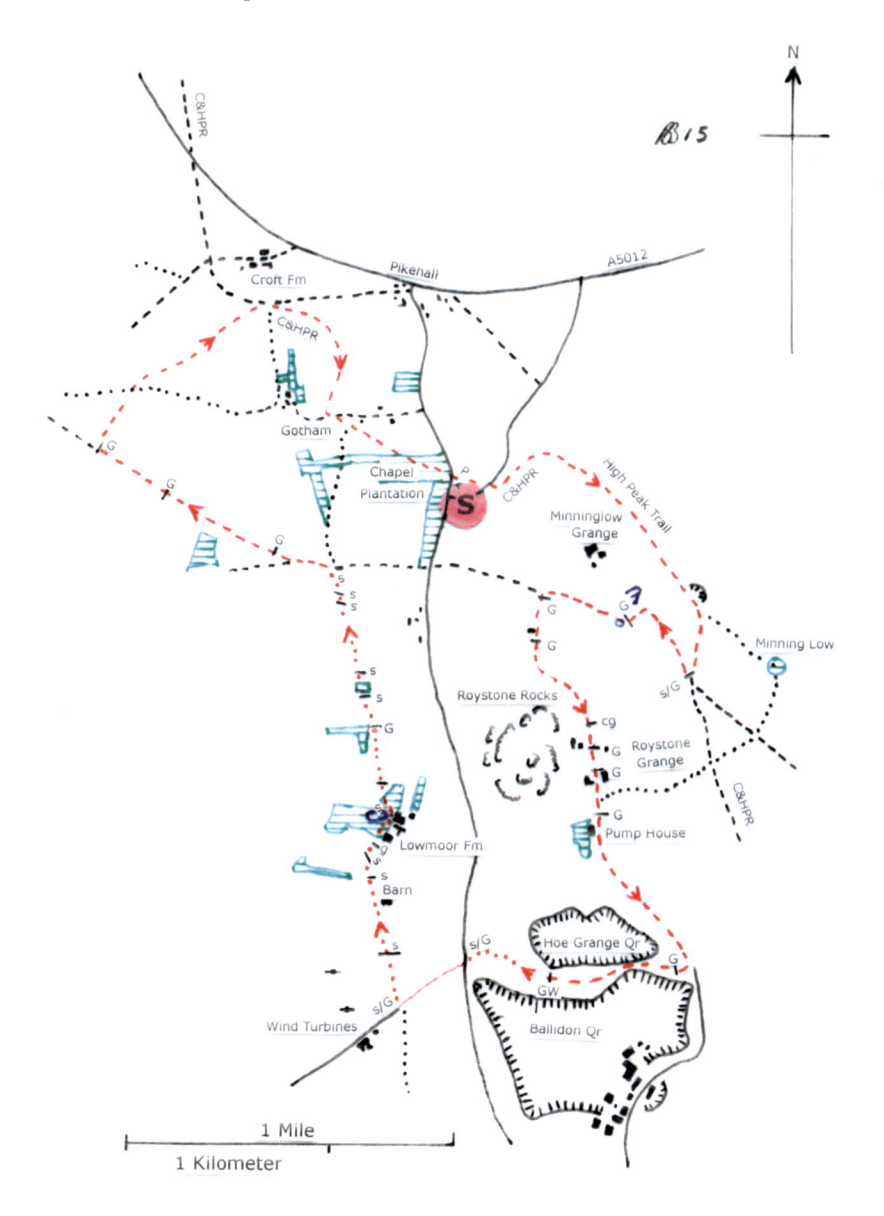

Walk 9   MINNINGLOW – ROYSTONE GRANGE

Route:
Minninglow Car Park – Roystone – Gotham – Minninglow Car Park
Distance:
8 miles (13km)
Difficulty:
Easy trail walking with field paths. Ascent/Descent 490ft (150m)
Start:
Minninglow Car Park. (SK 194 582)
Parking:
Free car parking with picnic tables. Turn south off the A5012 Newhaven – Cromford road at Pikehall. Turn left in half a mile after passing under the C&HPR bridge and then left again into the Minninglow car park.

Parts of this Walk and Walk 10 coincide with the Roystone Grange Trail for which there is an information booklet.

Minninglow Embankment

This is a walk passing through an area that has seen continuous human activity from Neolithic times to the present day. Up ahead is the instantly recognisable landmark of Minninglow Hill, the prominent tree cluster marking a typical Neolithic burial chamber involving large stone capping slabs and multiple chambers. This tumulus was excavated in 1851 by Thomas Bateman a famous local Archaeologist and Antiquary, and more recently by Barry Marsden in 1974.

Leave the car park in a SE direction to pass through the gates crossing Mouldridge Lane. (This was an un-gated level crossing that was particularly difficult for train drivers to see if approaching from the opposite direction, and they were instructed to halt before proceeding to cross.) Join the Trail, which soon crosses over the arched tunnel allowing access to Minninglow Grange seen down below on the right, adjacent to large silica sand pits. Also, look for the magnificent limestone embankment sited under Minninglow Hill. After approx. 200yds at the far end of the embankment, the line turns sharp right by a disused quarry before running straight along the hillside. On this stretch take the opportunity to look back at the embankment you have just crossed – one of the best examples of railway construction on the C&HPR. Half a mile further along you come to a cutting with the small Minninglow quarry on the left, still with its badly rusting crane, a reminder of another era.

Minninglow Quarry Crane

Bending R, note the old limekiln on the left before arriving at a bollard in the middle of the Trail. Here turn sharp R off the trail, down the sign-posted lane to 'Biggin, Cycle Route 548'. At the bottom the path turns sharp left to go past sand pits before bending right uphill to become Minninglow Lane. Walk up to the road junction and then turn L to Roystone Grange, first passing Roystone Cottages on the right. (Further down, a gate on the right allows entrance to the open access land surrounding Roystone rocks.)

Over a cattle grid and further on on the right is the site of 2nd century dwellings. The large irregular stone blocks that appear as base stones in the boundary walls for the farmyard are known as 'orthostats'. These characterise the Roman walls that are also encountered in other field boundaries in this area. Pass through the farmyard of Roystone Grange with its 18-19c buildings.) Further on you reach a building of church-like appearance on the right. This in fact was a Victorian pump house, which contained a huge steam driven compressor used to supply compressed air through cast iron pipes to quarries in the area to operate pneumatic drills. The only spring in the area was used as cooling water. In the same field and close by, is the site of a medieval farm run by the Cistercians who were also attracted to the site by the spring water. The site can be visited although there is not an awful lot to see. Further down the road the steep sided valley closes in on both sides.

Victorian Pump House, Roystone Grange

Quarry warning notices begin to appear on the right as the slope hides the presence of the operational Ballidon quarry. Just after the point where the road bends right, look for the gated path on the right where there is a wide expanse of grass verge. Turn R up this to pass between Ballidon quarry and its 'new' extension, aka Hoe Grange Quarry. At the narrowest point a useful information board explains the quarry workings and the layout of the plant. The high purity of the limestone and its practical use in so many industries has allowed expansion even though it lies with in the National Park. To accommodate environmental concerns, a tunnel has been made beneath the footpath to allow for the transportation of limestone through to the processing plant.

Minninglow Embankment

Carry on up the dale to reach an old disused limekiln on the left and a dew pond on the right. At this point turn up to the L of a wall towards the trees at the top. Here, Parwich Lane is reached at a T-junction. Go straight across and up the lane opposite to its crest where two small wind turbines come into view. Next, look out for a path crossing the road and go R over a stile by a gate into fields. Walk the length of two fields to pass to the left of an old barn. Carry on through two more fields to reach Lowmoor Farm below. Take the path that goes between the rear of the farm buildings and a large stagnant pond, exiting the farm over a stile into a lane turning L. Follow the track up right beside a small wood. Pass through the farm gate and cross an open field to the edge of Lowmoor Plantation. Leave the field by the gate. Now take left hand of two more gates, and continue to cross the next two fields to the left of the boundary wall. In the second field a small, deciduous copse is encountered. The way ahead is now straight, crossing six fields whose lateral boundaries are defined by broken walls. (Look out for two posted way-markers for direction). Eventually a wall stile marks the exit onto Minninglow Lane. Turn L here and then after approximately 250yds take the right fork at the lane intersection through a gate (National Cycle Network 548). Carry on up a gentle rise for about 1,100yds (1km) until a crossroads is reached. Here turn R on the track sign-posted 'Green Lane', down towards Pikehall.

The C&HPR/High Peak Trail is met again where it comes over an embankment from the left (signed PENNINE BRIDLEWAY Middleton Top 7½). At a four-way junction of paths, turn R onto the Trail. After two right-hand bends the famous Gotham curve begins, and as it turns sharp left it is bisected by the walled track that runs up from Gotham Grange.

The way ahead is now straight to the finish passing first through Chapel Plantation then over the Pikehall road to reach the car park.

Fish Bellied Rails

Gotham Curve

This is the sharpest curve on the whole line at 2.5 chains (165ft (50m) radius and extending round through 80°. It was also the tightest curve on the National British rail system. Gotham was always treated with great respect by the drivers, who had no wish for a derailment. To reduce this possibility, the track was banked and had a third check rail fitted on the inside. There was also an imposed speed limited of 5mph. Nevertheless the transit of the curve was a noisy operation as the wheel flanges ground and screeched against the rails. In the early days of the 4ft cast iron rails this transit was also a very bumpy experience as the curve was made up of 57 flats with each joint having an included angle of nearly 2°. In those days there would always be a stock of rails close by as fracture of this relatively brittle material was common.

Gotham Curve

Walk 10 Map

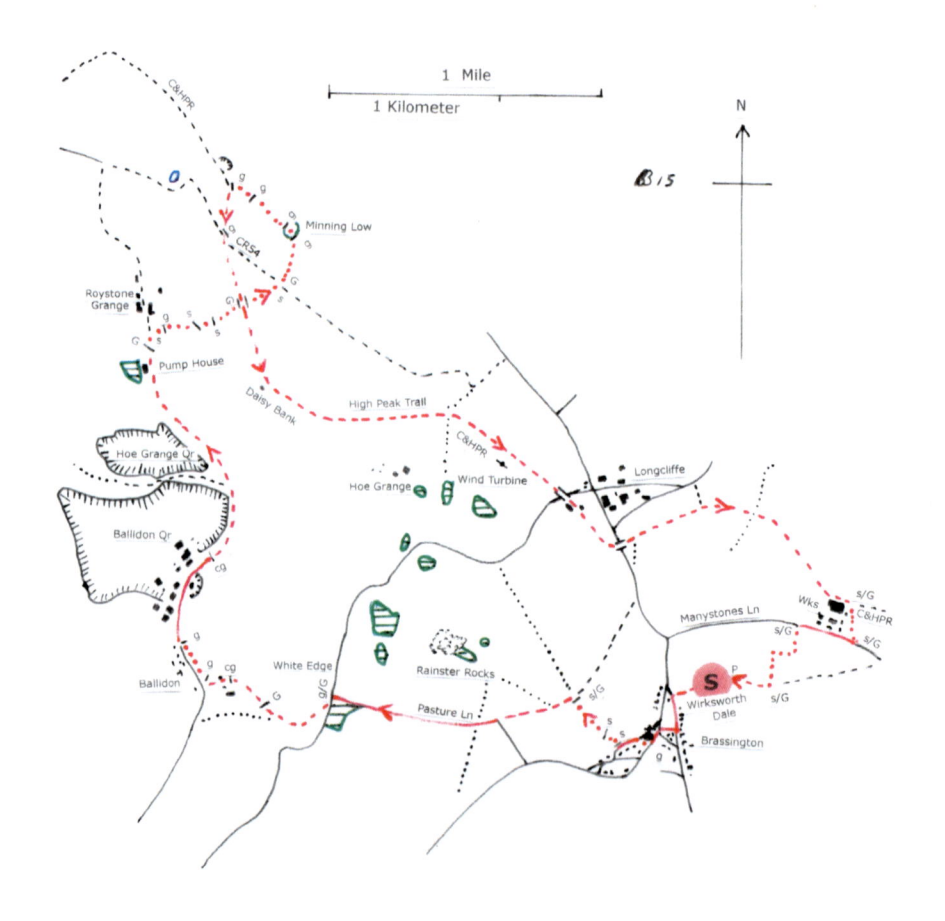

Walk 10   BRASSINGTON – LONGCLIFFE

Route:
Brassington – Ballidon – Roystone – Minninglow – Longcliffe – Brassington
Distance:
8.9 miles (14.3km)
Difficulty:
Easy walking with some field paths, involving 515 ft. (157m) of altitude change.
Start:
Car Park, Brassington. (SK 233 547)
Parking:
The free car park is on the northern outskirts of Brassington village and has picnic tables. It can be reached by turning south on the A5012 Newhaven – Cromford road at SK 218 590 or north on the B5035 Ashbourne – Wirksworth road at SK 234 522.

Brassington

Walk back down the car park access road (Wirksworth Dale) and turn L towards the ancient lead mining village of Brassington. After the Village Hall take the second road on the R (Maddock Lake), to meet the Miners Arms at the road junction. Turn R along Church Street beneath the imposing church of St James. The church contains many Norman features such as the tower and porch, and internally has some fine Ashford-in-the-Water 'Black Marble' columns.

At the end of the churchyard turn R through a gate and walk up past the gravestones to reach Hillside Lane. Turn L. In a short distance opposite Brown Top, take the stile R and follow the path uphill through two fields to reach the head of a green lane, which is part of the Limestone Way. At this point the top of Rainster Rocks comes into view looking NW. Turn L down the lane and when it is joined by a road from the left, it becomes Pasture Lane. Continue on to the T-junction with the B5056 and cross over to a gate. Now zigzag up the track and over the end of White Edge. Ignore the Limestone Way when it diverts left on its way to Parwich and stay on the track. Follow the track through a field gate with the village of Ballidon below. Go directly down to the village. On reaching the grass triangle at Cow Close Farm, take the fenced and gated public footpath on the right, behind the village notice board. This allows a safe passage around the bend, as this road is busy with heavy limestone trucks. On exiting the footpath keep to the right of the road. After approximately 300yds everything becomes very industrialised, with first a Concrete Block Manufacturer and then at the roundabout, the entrance to Ballidon Quarry. Keep on the (Roystone Lane) road, passing the weighbridge and then the crushing plant. Finally, peace is restored on reaching the cattle grid and the open access sign!

Follow the dale road up, keeping straight on past the old Victorian compressed air Pump House, and then take the first sign-posted stile R, situated on a right hand bend. After the first field, the footpath/track takes you up to the right of a boundary wall. Cross the wall at a signed stile and the route continues left of the wall before eventually breaking away to a gateway. (Note the round-roofed concrete building over on the left that was an explosives store for the local quarries). The route now goes directly up to pass through a tunnel under the C&HPR, and then straight on to reach Gallowlow Lane (not marked on OS) via a wall stile. Go straight across to follow the signed path (concession route) up to Minninglow. This prominent landmark is made up of a walled ring of trees that surround the tumulus, which is crowned by older taller trees.

Enter the tranquil site to see the large capping stones of a Neolithic barrow, which was excavated by Thomas Bateman in 1861.

Minninglow

Exit the site through the far gate NW and drop down the top field to a limestone clint outcrop with far-reaching views over the surrounding countryside. Carry on down the fields to reach the Trail at a gate adjacent to the old Minninglow Quarry.

Turn L and follow the Trail across the embankment passing an old limekiln on the left. Approx. 30yds after the bollard and footpath sign to Biggin, look for the remains of an early firebrick kiln on the right. This utilised the high silica sand brought up the lane from the pits at Minninglow Grange. Go straight ahead and pass through a cutting. After another cutting through a long straight section, the remote farm at Daisy Bank is seen on the right. On the steep slopes below, the

Romans cultivated the natural limestone terraces as allotments. The view to the S is now dominated by the quarrying complex at Ballidon. After a series of slow bends and straights the Trail passes out of the Peak Park. In another half mile the buildings of Longcliffe come into view. The extensive layout of the goods yard provided a loop bringing double tracks in over the B5056 by a steel girder bridge. The goods yard now houses picnic tables. (Note the interesting ironwork legs on one of the benches).

Longcliffe

This was an important and busy goods yard, which still retains its massive stone-built goods shed as well as the railway cottages. It was a site where water tenders were brought from Cromford. They were shunted up onto the ramp that is positioned on the south side of line and were then used for supplying locomotives and for commercial and domestic consumption. Coal was another import, with coal wharves positioned on a siding to the north. This siding continued on into a small quarry. Longcliffe was the railhead for the Buxton crews who, unlike their C&HPR colleagues, could work outside daylight hours. This meant they had the unenviable job of working through the night to distribute empty milk tanks and finally bring in the full ones on the early morning Manchester milk train.

Longcliffe

Longcliffe 1967

After a slight bend right the track then makes a sharp left turn through 90° at a radius of about 3 chains (198ft, (60m) to cross over the Brassington road. On the right are the remains of a disused quarry while down to the left is a conglomeration of industrial building adjacent to Longcliffe quarry. After the next right bend the Trail undertakes a wooded cutting, crossed at its far end by the Limestone Way. Carry on to the next right bend, with Harboro Rocks accompanied by a trig point ahead on the left, on the hill above. Note the remains of what was a mineral crushing plant on the hillside. Walk on to the mineral works, with its collection of green-sided corrugated buildings and hoppers. A recent addition to the complex skyline is four large wind turbines on Carsington Pasture.

Turn R off the Trail just after the works to reach Manystones Lane. Turn R along the lane, and after about 220yds take the signed stile L into fields, by a metal gate. Follow to the right of the boundary wall, turning R and then L. This is an area of extensive lead mining. The OS map tells that the mines had some interesting names: Bee Nest, Wester Head, Nickalum & Greatrake.

Finally on reaching a stile and gate you are in Wirksworth Dale again. Turn R to walk down to the car park and the end of the walk.

Walk 11 Map

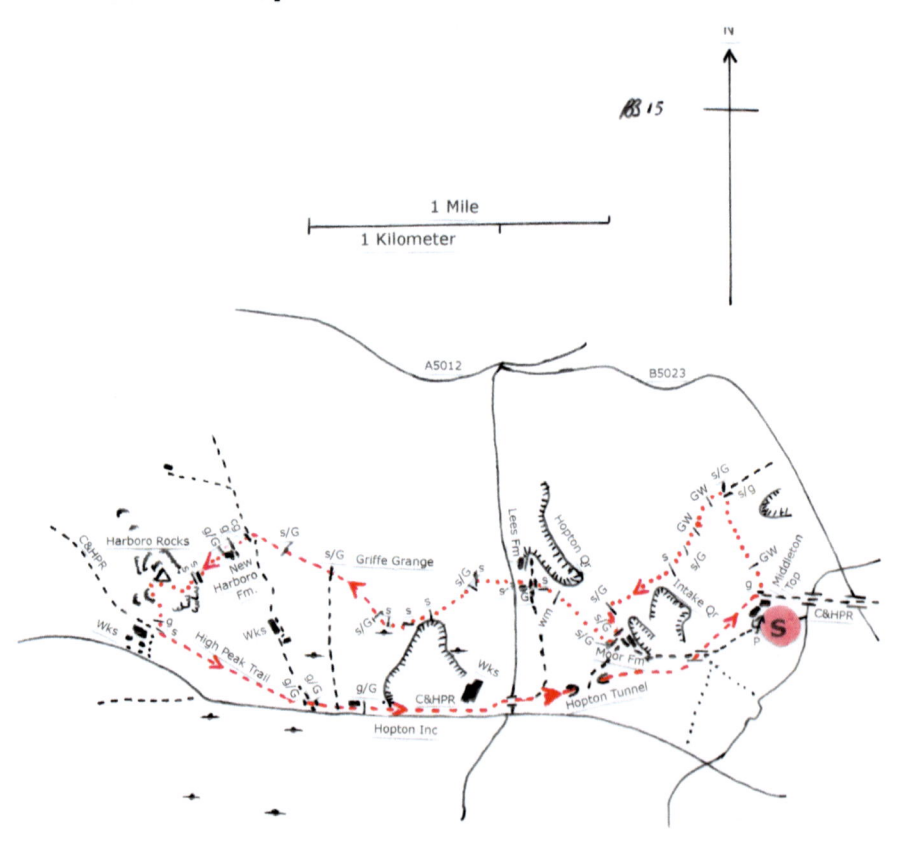

Walk 11

MIDDLETON TOP – HARBORO ROCKS

Route:
Middleton Top – Middleton Moor – Griffe Grange – Harboro Rocks – Hopton Incline – Middleton Top.
Distance:
5.6 miles (9km)
Difficulty:
Easy trail with some field walking involving 164ft. (50m) of altitude change.
Start:
Middleton Top car park. (SK 275 552)
Parking:
The car park is sign posted from the Cromford – Wirksworth road, B5035. The Pay & Display car park has toilets, picnic tables and a shop.

Hopton Top

Middleton Top's engine house chimney provides one of the most recognizable landmarks of the C&HPR. Inside the engine house is the only remaining winding engine on the line (out of eight built for the C&HPR) and this magnificent machine is kept in pristine working condition. Although now only driven by compressed air, it is an absolute 'must see' on its working days. Outside there are many interesting features, such as the wheel pit which functions when the engine is in motion, an open wooden wagon on line above the incline, an engine signaling board, the original semaphore signal, a cast iron track warning sign and a gradient indicator are in place. In front of the information centre is a fine run of five original fish bellied rails set out to clearly show the unique joining and fixing methods used.

Middleton Engine House

The walk starts from the rear of the visitors' centre. Cross the trail to find a signpost for 'Middleton Moor'. Proceed up the steps through a gate and then turn R to take the broad track through another gate up L onto the moor. Go straight up, and at the top of the rise note the large depression on the right, which is a legacy of the Middleton Limestone Mine collapsing some years ago. On reaching a green lane turn L and follow it a short distance to its end. Here go SW across three fields to arrive at the edge of Intake Quarry. Follow the boundary fence up and over, passing the capped shafts of numerous lead mines, before swinging R to meet a farm track. Now ahead of you is the imposing sight of seven wind turbines. Go L down the track to Moor Farm and turn R. Go R again with a finger post over a stile beside a field gate. Walk to the left of the boundary wall for a short way before bearing off L to a way marker post in a broken wall. Go down the field with Hopton Wood Quarry on the right. Exit the field by a squeeze stile to turn L through an arched bridge under the embankment that once carried the branch line up to the quarry. Walk down through Arm Lees Farm yard to cross the road.

Top of Hopton Incline

Go straight up the field to the right of the boundary wall, and at the top turn L at a stile by a gate. After another stile bear R to follow round the quarry boundary fence through two fields. Just before the end of the second field cross over a stile to climb left of the boundary wall to meet the quarry track, adjacent to the very large wind energy facility. Turn R and follow the track, which was once an ancient route of a portway. Climb over the hill of Griffe Grange and follow the track down passing a footpath sign to 'Hopton Top'. After approx. 400yds look for a waymarker on the right and turn L across the cattle grid keeping to the left of the drystone wall up to 'New Harboro Farm'. Pass through the gate and alongside the farm buildings to a gateway. Go straight uphill through a couple of wall stiles before crossing open grassland leading on to the dolomitic limestone outcrop of Harboro Rocks. The path bears to the right before dropping down to the High Peak Tail. However it is worth diverting to the trig point (OS S4140, height 1,243ft (379m)) to enjoy the panoramic views north across the White Peak and south to Carsington Water, now with its accompanying wind turbines on Carsington Pasture. On leaving the top head SW down towards the chemical / mineral works.

At the bottom turn L onto the Trail, proceeding over a stone-faced embankment before reaching a cutting. At its end pass through the gated crossing of the access road to the Sibelco works. As the track now bends left it is joined by Manystones Lane, which runs parallel with it, as it descends Hopton Incline. Cross the bridle way to Grange Mill to arrive at Engine Man's Cottage, now with picnic tables. At the top of the incline is a modern sculpture incorporating one of the original cast iron rails (look underneath). Behind this was once positioned the engine house and reservoir. The nearby information board provides a picture of a much-photographed scene as an uphill train tackles the incline under full steam.

Hopton Incline
Length = 1,371 ft
Gradient = 1 in 14
Altitude: Top = 1067ft, Bottom = 952ft, Elevation = 115ft
From 1831 to 1877 a stationary steam-winding engine operated a continuous chain haulage loop as on the other inclines.
In 1877 the gradient was eased top and bottom to 1:60, 1:30, 1:20, 1:14 (600ft (183m), 1:470 so that the locomotives and wagons could freely run the incline.

Passing through the gates set off down the incline, and just before reaching the Plate Layers Hut, note on the left the sidings that ran back to a tipping dock for the Bone Works that once operated here.

Hopton Incline

After the hut the track passes over an arched bridge, which gave road access to the works.

Just beyond the foot of the incline is the site of a tragic accident, which occurred on the 6th October 1937. A train, making a high speed run at the incline, spread the lines and then derailed and rolled down the embankment onto the road. Sadly the driver, Mr Boden, was killed.

The embankment now bends left passing over the Wirksworth to Via Gellia road.

Close by on the right and below the embankment, look for the abandoned boiler and engine base that was used to haul wagons up from Hopton Wood Quarry. The engine was installed as a stationary unit with the haulage cable passing under the C&HP line.

A long limestone cutting is now entered leading to the Hopton Tunnel (Length, 339ft (111m).

Hopton Tunnel 2016

Hopton Tunnel

Next, the line emerges into a shorter cutting before the track bears right over an embankment. Adjacent to the double gate, the sidings of Intake Quarry branched off to the left.

Soon, the 80ft tall brick chimney of Middleton Top Engine House comes into view and the end of the walk is reached over another embankment dominated by the Intake Quarry spoil heaps.

Middleton Top Engine House

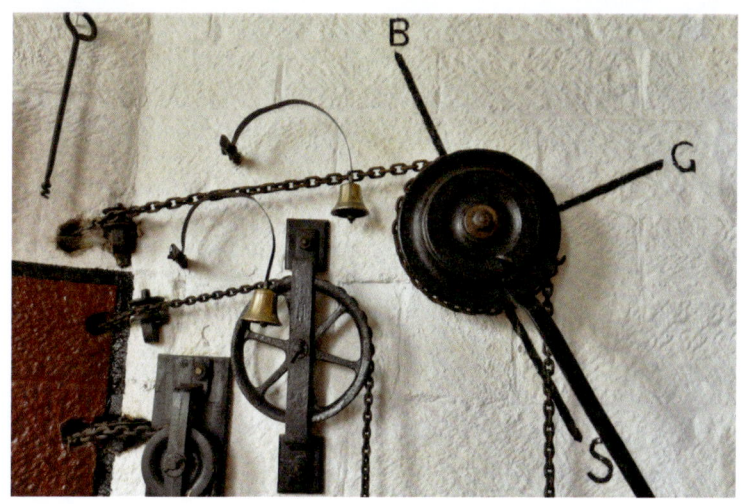

Wagon Motion Indicator

Walk 12 Map

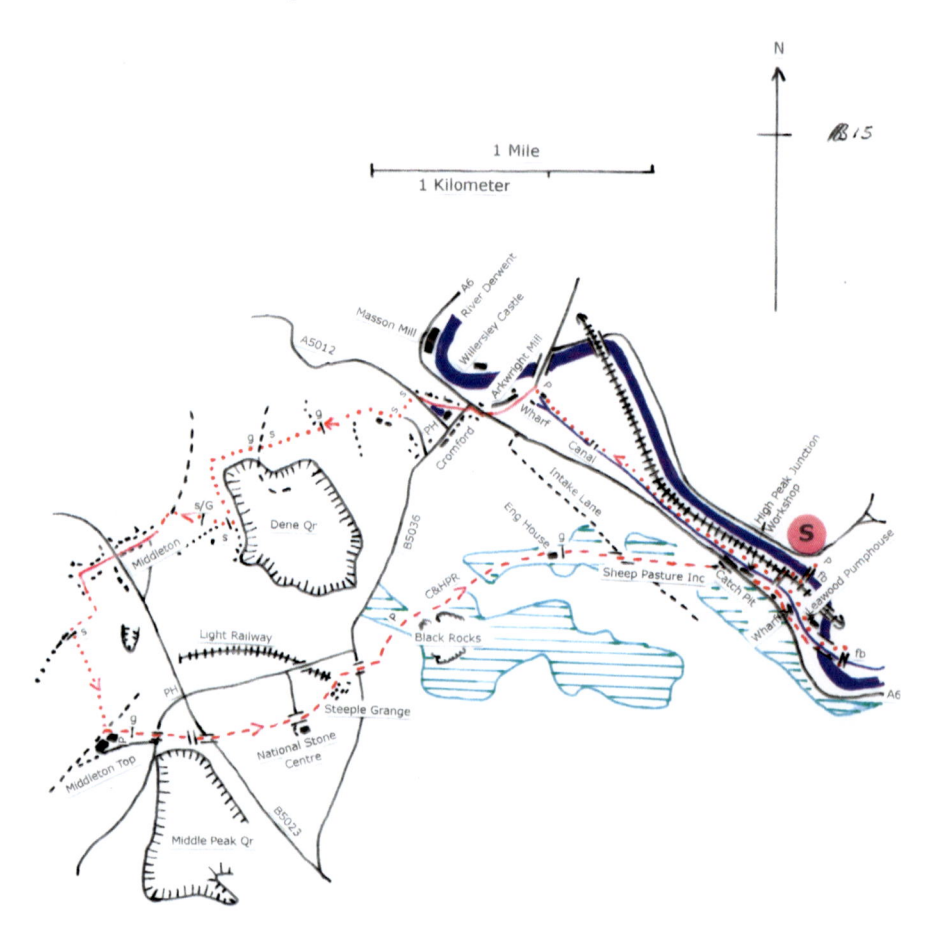

Walk 12   HIGH PEAK JUNCTION - MIDDLETON TOP

Route:
High Peak Junction – Cromford – Middleton Top – Middleton Incline – Steeple Grange – Black Rocks – Sheep Pasture Incline – High Peak Junction – Cromford Wharf – Lea Wood Pumping Station – High Peak Junction.

Distance:
7.38 miles (11.9km)

Difficulty:
Easy trail and towpath walking with steep descent and ascent over an altitude of 820ft (250m)

Start:
High Peak Junction car park (SK 315 561).

Parking:
Take the minor road from the Cromford traffic lights signed to Cromford Mill & Crich. Cross over the River Derwent and take the right fork to pass under the railway close to the station. Follow the road for a mile along the banks of the river to find the car park on the right.

High Peak Junction

Cromford Workshops

Take the footpath R at the end of the Car Park to cross the footbridge over the River Derwent. After the sewage works go L over the railway bridge and the canal bridge to reach the once busy Cromford Goods Yard with its offices and workshops. Here you will find an information centre, shop, toilets and picnic tables.

The workshop is well worth visiting as it has been restored to its original layout and contains the only remaining cast-iron rails still in situ, bordering the inspection pit. The workshop was reported to have assembled a locomotive as early as 1834. In the early days experimental designs were common with the components being bought for assembly under the guidance of the resident engineer. It should be noted that the OS map and the information boards refer incorrectly to this as being High Peak Junction whereas in railway terms the junction is ¾ mile south east of here. The spur to the junction from here was built in 1853 to connect the C&HPR into the main line network.

Follow the canal towpath NW, that is with the railway and river on your right. After about a mile the canal terminates at the Cromford basin in front of the world famous Cromford Mill built by Sir Richard Arkwright. The Pay & Display car park on the right contains toilets and picnic tables and the second of the wharf buildings on the left is now a café.

> ### Cromford Mill
> Following the success of his horse powered mill in Nottingham, Richard Arkwright came to Cromford in 1771 to build a water-powered cotton-spinning mill, the first in the world. He had invented a cotton-spinning machine called a Water Frame for the mass production of cotton thread, thereby introducing the factory system that became the model for the industrial revolution. Arkwright had been attracted to the small, secluded village of Cromford because the local lead mining industry had produced a constant supply of water from its drainage system known as a sough. Also, in the early days, he wanted to keep secret his revolutionary new technology. Arkwright was a model employer and although he employed children as young as seven he preferred to employ families rather than the parish poor. His wages were good and higher than agricultural workers at that time. For his workforce he built good stone houses and provided shops, a school, a chapel and a church. The factory worked a daily two 12-hour shift and a six-day working week.

Turn L along the pavement of Mill Road, pass the car park and then take the first turning L (signed 'PRIVATE DRIVE'. Just before the gate turn R past the cast iron bollard to follow the enclosed walled footpath up to the main road (A6). Turn R and walk down to the traffic lights of this busy junction. The aim is to cross diagonally, so go directly over Mill Road and then follow the little 'green man' left and right to the opposite corner. Then turn L to walk the short distance into Cromford Market Square and The Greyhound Hotel. Arkwright built the hotel in 1778 for his many visitors who came from all over the world to see his factory. It was also used for Board meetings.

Take the narrow road on the right of the Greyhound, passing the Boat Inn and the Post Office en route to a large millpond on the left. Carry on to the road junction adjacent to a garage. Cross over the road and climb up the footpath opposite. At the end of the first section of handrail turn R to pass in front of a row of houses. After the estate road-end carry on up the path, passing Derbyshire Wildlife Trust Nature Reserve signs on both sides along the way. Eventually, after a steady, uphill climb, the path meets a gate to enter farmland. Walk up the field, and via a wooded green lane you finally arrive at a stile onto the access road to Dene Quarry.

Go directly over the road and L through the gate and squeeze stile opposite. Follow the path along the northern edge of the quarry, which soon takes a 90 degree turn left. Halfway along this edge, turn off R over a fence stile to walk up a walled track away from the quarry. In a short way the path splits. Bear R away from the barn to a gate/stile and then up a green lane. Follow this path for about 100yds to a T-junction. Turn L and go straight ahead down the track that leads into Middleton.

At the road junction with the Methodist church on the corner, cross over New Road and walk steeply up Water Lane. When the road starts to bend right, turn off L up Moor Road. Passing a finger post, the track turns sharp right and up onto Middleton Moor. Just before a gate/stile, turn off L over a stile and walk directly across the fields to Middleton Top.

At the top of the incline is an open wooden wagon on a portion of reconstructed track, a signalling indicator and a lower quadrant signal. On descending the incline the first bridge under was built in 1980 to accommodate the site traffic involved in the construction of Carsington Water reservoir while the next is the older road up to Intake Quarry.

Descend the incline. A sign on the right invites one to take a 200yd detour to the delights of the Rising Sun Inn. Soon the rock cutting is spanned by an impressive high-arched stone bridge carrying the old Middleton to Wirksworth road.

Further down, the new road is passed over before the wheel pit is reached at the bottom. The accompanying information board explains how the wheel could be adjusted to take into account the continued expansion and contraction that occurs due to the normal fluctuations in ambient temperature. The thermal expansion that occurs on such long lengths of steel rope is significant.

Middleton Incline

Length = 2,124 ft
Incline = 1 in 8.25
Altitude Top = 1,001ft, Bottom = 722ft, Elevation = 279ft
The winding engine is the sole survivor of the eight provided for the line in 1925-29,
manufactured by the Butterley Iron Works, of Butterley, Derbyshire. The engine is of a two-cylinder low-pressure condensing beam type. The cylinders are 25in bore with 60in. stroke.
The cast iron flywheel is 14ft in diameter. The drive to the rope pulley is from a pinion on the engine crankshaft to a gearwheel producing a reduction of 1:2.75.

Originally the engine was driven by two wood-fired Lancashire boilers, which were replaced by two Cornish boilers in about 1868. These are now defunct and the engines now run on compressed air for demonstration purposes. The bell and pointer control signals used to communicated between the bottom and top of the incline are on display in the engine house. They had three positions 'B' for Stand By, 'G' for Go, and 'S' for Stop.

Middleton Incline

On the right of the pit was the Middlepeak Quarry siding with its coal wharf, blacksmiths shop and other railway buildings. After passing a retaining embankment on the right a wall indicates the point where a proposed incline plane of 1:13 gradient was to be built to connect the C&HPR to the Midland Railway at Wirksworth. Although work was started on the engine house the project was never completed.

The Trail passes a number of small quarries before you arrive at the National Stone Centre on the right.

In the car park opposite sits a strange looking engine that is in need of some care and attention. It is RS8 that was built in ICI's Tunstead workshops in 1960 using the frame of a 0-4-0 saddle-tank engine originally built in 1923 and a diesel-hydraulic engine supplied by Roll-Royce.

After the line bends left Steeplehouse Quarry is reached.

Here there was a small goods yard with an office, coal stack and a stable. In 1955 vandals opened the points into the goods yard, which deposited an 0-4-0 saddle tank engine down the embankment into a cottage garden. Fortunately no one was injured.

Steeplehouse Accident 1955

On the left as the line turns right was the Killers Branch, which climbed for half-mile up to Middleton Quarries on an incline of 1 in 27. This is now the site of Steeple Grange Light Railway Company, who operate public rides at selected times through out the year on their 18in gauge line.

The Trail now crosses the valley on an impressive stone-faced embankment to reach the Black Rocks picnic site with toilets, picnic tables and refreshment kiosk. Next to the visitors centre are the remains of Cromford Moor Lead Mines. On the right a track leads up onto the Black Rocks outcrop, which is worth a detour on a nice day for its spectacular views. The gritstone rock was quarried and a tramway brought the stone down to a loading dock on its own siding. Note the cast iron L&NWR boundary markers.

This level section of track contours right round Cromford Moor passing first on the left a 22 mile distance indicator, and then a corrugated-iron shed. Just before arriving at the top of Sheep Pasture incline the site of three reservoirs for feeding the winding engine can be seen on the right while on the opposite side there a magnificent view down on to Cromford and Matlock. An information board explains the significance of the various buildings related to one of the great names in the industrial revolution, Sir Richard Arkwright. The engine house stands intact but empty. The missing chimney was remotely positioned up on the rocks behind and connected by a flue cut through the rocks.

Sheep Pasture Incline

When open in 1831 this incline was operated as two, Cromford and Sheep Pasture, and involved two stationary steam-winding engines.
Sheep Pasture: Length = 2133ft, Gradient = 1 in 8.25
Cromford: Length = 1740ft, Gradient = 1 in 8.5
In 1857 the inclines were combined to form the present Sheep Pasture Incline.
Altitude: Top = 755ft, Bottom = 295ft, Elevation = 460ft
Sheep Pasture is unique in that it is the only incline to be fitted with a catch pit. The reason for this is that there is no natural run off at the bottom, the line turning sharply right in the Goods Yard. On the 1st March 1888, on the last run of the day, a brake van and a loaded limestone wagon ran away.

On reaching an estimated terminal velocity of 120 mph (193kph) they went straight off the track at the bottom and cleared both the canal and the main railway line to end up wrecked in the fields beyond. The points at the Catch Pit were spring loaded open and it was the job of the points man to close them for the descending and ascending wagons. The speed of the descending loads could be judged from the sequence of gongs operated in his cabin by wires attached to treadles depressed by the wagon wheel flanges.

Sheep Pasture Engine House

On descending the incline, the first feature to be encountered is an old quarry on the right that contains a three-legged jib crane used for handling large blocks of stone. Just below this is a bridge under for the passage of Intake lane.

The next big cutting was the site of the Cromford Top Engine House. The track bed would have been flat at this point to allow for easy changing-over of wagons. The amalgamation of inclines necessitated the regrading of the line and the introduction of a right curve. Proceeding down onto the final straight reveals a catch pit with its contents of broken wagons as testament to its usefulness.

Take time to stop and look at the Catch Pit before passing under the A6 where the bridge was rebuilt to cope with modern day traffic. You then arrive at Cromford Goods Yard, which is now called the High Peak Junction Workshops.

The first building on the left is the workshop positioned beside the wheel pit while on the opposite side is the spring fed water tank that supplied the water tankers servicing the quarries and residents up on the limestone plateau of the White Peak.

Next to this is some relayed track with a couple of brake vans that can be visited to inspect their information boards.

Moving on from the workshop, and bearing R, the first long building beside the track is the railway store. This is followed by a small building which was the Weighbridge Office. Just in front of the wharf shed with its overhanging canopy the white post beside the canal indicates the remains of a 5 ton crane, while a wagon-loading gauge next to the shed is suspended from a beam above the track. At the bottom of the lane coming in from the right is the Goods Office. The level crossing at this point was controlled by a very crude banner signal that consisted of a single sheet of iron that could be swung round a pole.

Wharf Shed

Carry straight on, ignoring the lane on the right. At the gate is where the spur was built in 1853 to connect into the main line. Turn L here and go on the towpath for just over 150 yards to cross the canal by the swing bridge (No.6). Walk back down the side of the canal (sign post to 'High Peak Junction') to pass above Lea Wood Pumphouse. If open, this magnificent engine is well worth visiting (see note below).

It is now just a short way back to Cromford Goods Yard, and the end of the walk.

> **Cromford Canal**
> The Cromford Canal was opened in 1794 and was built by Benjamin Outram and William Jessop initially to serve Arkwright Mill at Cromford. When the C&HPR arrived in 1831 the canal traffic increased significantly with coal, cotton, limestone and gritstone being the most important goods. However when the C&HPR was connected into the national rail network in 1853 the canal traffic started to decline. In 1900 the Butterley tunnel closed because of mining subsidence, and the canal closed entirely in 1942.

Cromford Canal

Leawood Pumphouse

All canal systems need water replenishment systems to compensate for loss through lock systems. In this case it was the flight of fourteen locks at Langley Mill where the Cromford Canal connected to the Erewash. Although initially serviced by the lead mine drainage of Bonsal and Cromford soughs, later mining development led to water shortages affecting the water levels in the canal. Hence in 1849 this pumping house became operational, transferring water from the river to the canal. Because the extraction of water from the River Derwent was controlled by an act of Parliament to protect the water-powered cotton mills using it, water extraction could only take place between 8pm on Saturday and 8pm on Sunday.

Accordingly, this single cylinder steam beam engine was designed to lift a pump plunger of 15tons plus 4 tons of water per stroke at a speed of 7 strokes per minute. This meant that over 39,00 tons could be lifted in 24 hours. Fortunately this beautiful engine is maintained in operational steam condition by a dedicated band of volunteers. Although the engine is the main attraction here, just note the quality of building design from an era that took pride in the smallest detail.

Leawood Pumphouse

Acknowledgements

Firstly, a big thank you to all our friends in the Chapel-en-le-Frith Rambling Club who acted as guinea pigs walking the line from Whaley Bridge to Cromford in eight walks between 2006 and 2008. Their questions and suggestions were invaluable. A particular thank you to our walking companion Les Jones who has accompanied us on our many walks since then, as we have gradually refined the routes.

Most of the historic facts about the railway are gleaned from the sources named in the References Section (page 101) for which we are deeply indebted. We have met many C&HPR enthusiasts along the journey and we are pleased to have spent some time in the company of the late Norman Taylor, ex C&HPR driver, listening to his many stories of life on the line.

Also, we would like to pay tribute to the efforts of many people employed within the various authorities who have been instrumental in preserving and extending access to the line, supporting the infrastructure and increasing public knowledge thereby achieving what we have today: Derbyshire County Council; Peak District National Park Authority; High Peak Borough Council and Whaley Bridge Town Council. Particular thanks go to the following: Colin Goodwin, Middleton Top engineman; Michael Bentley, Buxton Shed engineman; Andy Pollock, ex Head Ranger DCC; Rick Jillings, Assistant Area Manager DCC Countryside Services; Claire O'Reilly, Senior Project Officer DCC Pedal Peak II; Stephanie Rayboult, Town Clerk WBTC and John Pritchard, Councillor WBTC.

As can be seen from the fine black and white photographs that accompany the walks, we have been extremely lucky and privileged to have ready access to the extensive photo archive of the late ER Morten by kind permission of his son John. For the picture of the Gunpowder Mill at Fernilee by Inkerman Hill, 1911, we acknowledge the help of Chris Simpson of Courtyard Publicity and Chris Helm (the photograph's keeper). For the photograph of the ruined mill in front of the dam construction, we thank Ni Rowlands of Whaley Bridge History Society. Finally, thanks also go to Sue Lake for her professional and forensic editing. And, last but not least, a big thank you to Thelma and Wendy for their unwavering support, not forgetting the packed lunches…

References

The Cromford & High Peak Railway by A Rimmer. Published by The Oakwood Press.
ISBN 0 85361 319 2

The Cromford & High Peak Railway by John Marshall. Published by Martin Bairstow : Revised Edition Featuring Wirksworth and Steeple Grange
ISBN 9 781871 944396

Scenes From The Past : 37 (PART ONE), Railways of the High Peak, Whaley Bridge to Friden
by N Jones & JM Bentley. Published by Foxline.
ISBN 10 1 870119 62 2

Scenes from the Past : 37 (PART TWO), Onwards to Cromford & High Peak Junction
by N Jones & JM Bentley. Published by Foxline.
ISBN 10 1 870119 67 3

Scenes from the Past : 50 The Buxton Line (PART ONE) Stockport to Whaley Bridge by Gregory K Fox. Published by Foxline.
ISBN 1 870119 85 1

Scenes from the past : 32. Buxton to Ashbourne. by JM Bentley & GK Fox. Published by Foxline.
ISBN 1 8701 1945 2

The Coal Mines of Buxton by AF Roberts and JT Leach. Published by Scarthin Books.
ISBN 978 0 90775 810 5

The Gunpowder Mills of Fernilee by Joyce Winfield.

Places of Interest

Middleton Top Engine House
This is the C&HPR's crown jewel. The beautifully restored 40hp steam engine was built by the Butterley Company in 1829 and is the worlds oldest working rotative beam engine in its original engine house. There were six similar engines for use on the steepest of the nine inclines that had stationary engines for transporting the wagons up and down the track. The engine, which is now powered by compressed air, is open to visitors on selected Sundays and Bank holiday Mondays.
For further details contact:
Tel: 01629 823204
www.derbyshire.gov.uk/countryside/leisure

High Peak Junction Workshop
The workshop, typical of the 19c, is complete with forge and tools of the period and replicates contemporary pictures of the room. Here in the early days of the railway the first crude locomotives were built and serviced as well as the manufacture of miles of chains for the inclined planes. The workshop, shop and information centre is open at weekends and Bank Holiday weeks.

Leawood Pump House
This magnificent 70hp steam beam engine was built in 1849 to pump water from the River Derwent into the Cromford Canal. This had become necessary because the canal's water supply from mine drainage had become unreliable. As the water of the River Derwent was extremely important for the cotton mills of the valley, the extraction of water was restricted to a 24-hour period between 8pm Saturday and 8pm Sunday. To achieve this a giant pump was installed that could lift 4 tons of water per stroke. At seven strokes per minute a total of 39,000 tons could be removed in the allotted time. The engine is driven by live steam generated by two Lancashire boilers. The Pump House is open to visitors on selected Sundays, weekends and Bank Holiday Mondays.
For further details:
Tel: 01629 823204
www.derbyshire.gov.uk/countryside/leisure

Cromford Mill

Richard Arkwright, the inventor of the Water Frame cotton-spinning machine for the mass production of cotton thread, moved to Cromford in 1771. Here, in what was then a small remote village, Arkwright established what was to be the world's first water-powered cotton spinning mill. This site was selected because it had a good reliable water supply and it was positioned on a main packhorse route. Its seclusion was also useful in keeping the invention a secret. Arkwright became rich and successful, allowing him to build further mills on the site. The complex is now a World Heritage site and is open to the public 9am to 5pm daily except Christmas Day.

The Steeple Grange Light Railway

The SGLR is an 18in gauge line built on the track bed of the half-mile Killers branch of the C&HPR that served Middleton Quarry. The branch contained a 1,110 yard section of 1 in 27 gradient that proved a tricky descent for a fully loaded limestone train and runaways were not unknown. Motive power these days is provided by diesels, battery-electric and petrol locomotives, and passengers are carried on manriders salvaged from Bevercotes Colliery in Nottinghamshire. The railway operates between 12.00 noon and 5.00pm Sundays and Bank Holidays from Easter to October, also Saturdays in July, August and September.
www.steeplegrange.co.uk

Cromford & High Peak Railway 1831

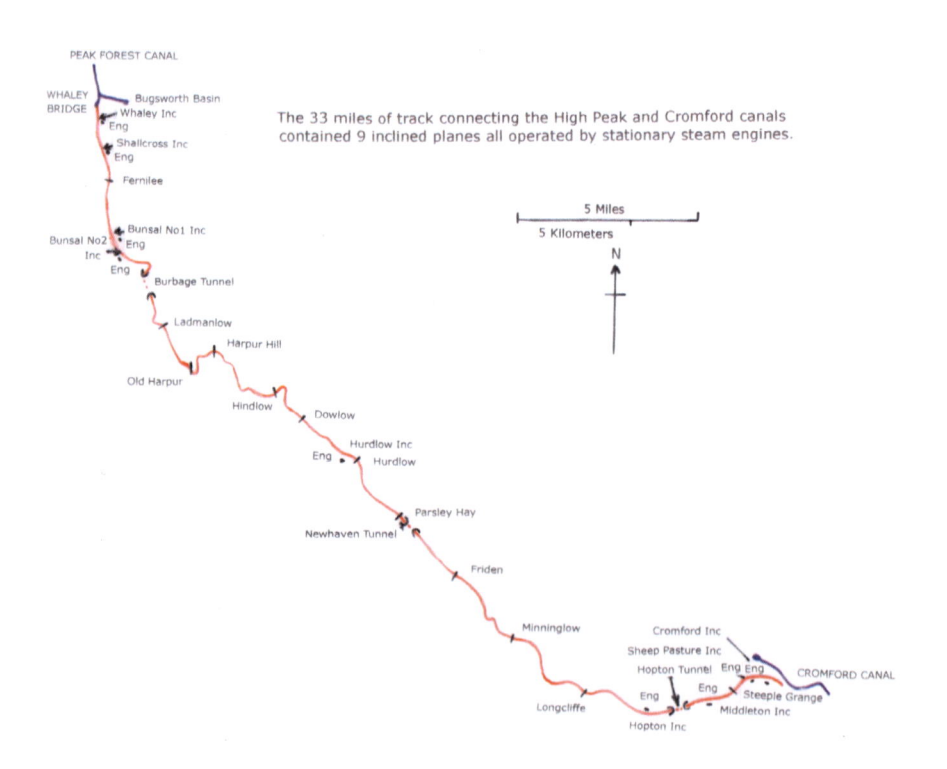

The 33 miles of track connecting the High Peak and Cromford canals contained 9 inclined planes all operated by stationary steam engines.